The Minack Open-Air Theatre

THE MINACK OPEN-AIR THEATRE

A symposium edited by
AVERIL DEMUTH

DAVID & CHARLES: NEWTON ABBOT

7153 4254 1

Printed in Great Britain by
Latimer Trend & Company Limited Plymouth
for David & Charles (Holdings) Limited
South Devon House Newton Abbot Devon

Contents

List of Illustrations

Illustrations

Prologue

O ver so many years thanks are due to so many people for all manner of aid that it would be difficult to name them all. People have given encouragement, criticism, labour, and money; have written plays, arranged and directed music, made costumes, shepherded the audience, and managed the business side; but above all for honourable mention come the various companies of players, with their directors, who have endured the worst the Minack can do in order to give their best to our loyal audiences.

ROWENA CADE

CHAPTER 1

The Story of the Minack

AVERIL DEMUTH

M any years ago I was climbing slowly up the cliff from
the Minack Theatre, not because the path in those days
was much steeper and more slippery than it is now, but
because I was so intrigued by the conversation of a party of
sightseers coming up behind me. It was single-line traffic and
only the very young and agile could by-pass a slow climber going
up or down. This time the people behind me, who had been
viewing the theatre that afternoon, were in no hurry, as their
chattiest member frequently stopped for breath to expound on
Cornish lore and legend in general, and the origin of the Minack
Theatre in particular. One of the girls in the party, turning to
look down on the grass-covered stage and graceful 'broken'
pillars, wondered aloud how the theatre came into existence in
such a seemingly inaccessible place; to which the cicerone in
lordly terms replied, 'Well, there's been a theatre of sorts here
ever since the time of the Romans, of course.' Now, when one
passes the box office and descends the wide, easy path to the
corner where the theatre itself suddenly comes into full view, it
is hard to picture it as it was in the days before the last war, and
the mind baulks at the thought of building any sort of stage on
such an improbable site. Nor does Miss Rowena Cade, whose
vision inspired the project and whose hands built the theatre we
see today, date from the time of the Romans. In fact, had those
sightseers visited the spot in 1930, they would have found

11

nothing but a steep slope of cliff, like thousands of others along the coasts of Cornwall, where bracken, furze, brambles and coarse grass ended abruptly in rocks, cave, and sea.

Minack is the name of the massive rock below the theatre jutting out into the sea, and always on summer evenings there will be patient fishermen down there, a sure distraction if the play of the moment fails to hold the attention. Once during a very long, very wordy classical drama an audible sigh of satisfaction went up from the audience above when a man on the rock below landed a sizeable catch. There seems to be a certain amount of controversy as to how Minack should be pronounced. The highbrows favour My-nack, and the locals call it Minnick. If the name derives from the Anglo-Saxon foundation of monks and nuns, known to have existed in the nearby village of St Buryan, they would have called themselves *munachs* and *minni-kins* in their own language, and it seems that Minnick is most likely to be correct. In St Just, nine miles away, I have overheard local fishermen arranging a rendezvous for 'Minnick, Saturday, all being well'. And Minnick is the pronunciation which Miss Cade herself prefers.

From the box office—the pillbox left from the last war—one looks down on the crowds on Porthcurno beach and the jade green sea dotted with shouting bathers, and it is hard to realise that in the 1920s, era of *The Boy Friend*, the bay was practically empty; and what is now a paradise for summer holidaymakers was then a deserted little white sand cove which was, unofficially, the exclusive property of the Eastern Telegraph Company. Furthermore, the proprieties were so strictly observed that ladies were expected to keep to the left side of the beach, which had the sun, while the men had the Minack side, where a splendid diving board was fixed to the rocks. I have a snapshot of myself going off the board, and one of my parents, comfortably propped against a boulder under my mother's sunshade, both of them peacefully sleeping on a peacefully empty beach. Today, the car park in the valley is often full up in August and to find a corner of the beach quiet enough for sleep would be hard indeed; some 20,000 people attend the summer season of plays, and the Minack Theatre itself has changed out of all recognition from its first emergence from the Porthcurno cliffs.

In 1929 a company of local amateurs staged *A Midsummer Night's Dream* in a sylvan setting a short distance inland from Porthcurno. The music was provided by the Penzance Orchestral Society—still going strong—and to judge from photographs and reminiscences the production must have been a sheer delight, and possibly closer to Shakespeare's own conception than many of the highly sophisticated, often bizarre productions of recent years. The moving spirit in these early days was Dorothea Valentine, a very able woman who had been a schoolteacher, but was then looking after her elderly parents at St Levan Rectory. She was drama-minded, and used to attend all the village concert shows given in the Eastern Telegraph Company's hall, and at once recognised the acting potential of the Cornish. Having seen the sets and costumes that Miss Cade had made for scenes from *Alice in Wonderland*, given in the old Pavilion in Penzance, Miss Valentine decided that 'the Minack lot' should all be dragged into a follow-up of *The Dream*. Miss Cade vows that they would never have bothered about plays if left to themselves, but with all the enthusiasm of success, after *The Dream*, Miss Valentine's company of players decided to move from the wooded meadow which was such a perfect setting for that particular play, to the cliff garden of Minack House, where they would give *The Tempest*.

Unfortunately the garden proved unsuitable in many ways, the main drawback being the lack of seating space for an audience, that integral and essential part of any play. Another site was considered on the far side of Porthcurno Bay; the shape was suitable, but to turn it into a theatre would have meant draining a bog before any work on it could be begun. By this time Miss Cade's interest was really roused, and she decided to build a terrace at the bottom of the gully next to her cliff garden. The granite outcrops on either side would make 'wings', and the fact that there was a huge mass of moorstone in the middle of the slope—roughly on a level with what is now the front row of seats—deterred her not at all. The moorstone must be moved, and the slight natural curve of the slope could be tiered to seat an audience, and for a stage backcloth they would have the Logan Rock, the sweep of Lizard Light, and the sea itself. What more perfect setting for *The Tempest* could there be?

To lesser mortals the task of building a theatre in such a position seems too intimidating to contemplate, but when one looks at the stage that stands today on the original terrace one can only think of Rowena Cade as one of the Olympians. With the help of Charles Thomas Angove and William Rawlings—dear, gruff, faithful Billy who for so many years worked with her on the construction, and, when through failing health he could not longer take an active part, organised the car park in latter years, greeting old friends with a wealth of lusty Cornish idiom—these three laboured on the stage during the winter months of 1931–2, and by May the levelled terrace was built and turfed, a few dry-walled, turfed tiers of seats were made for the audience in the slope of the cliff, and in August of 1932, in perfect weather, the local amateur company staged its production of *The Tempest*, and the Minack Theatre was born.

Seeing the theatre as it is today, it is almost impossible to imagine the staggering task that confronted the three builders with that first terrace-stage. From the granite boulders on the cliffs the men cut stone to face up the terrace, which was made where the grass of the slope ended and the ground fell away sheer into a 70-ft deep zawn, a sea-filled rift in the cliffs. Filling of earth and small stones for the stone-courses had to be brought down the muddy, slippery little path normally used only for the disposal of household rubbish in the zawn—those were the days before the dust carts came round the country districts—or the filling was thrown down with a shovel from the ledges up above. Miss Cade records that all material was precious, and that only one wheelbarrow and a few rocks were lost overboard. But she says that when she was making the big throne she left some reinforcement wire over the back and seat and weighted it

14

down with a 12 lb sledge-hammer, but the wind in the night was so strong that it blew the netting and the hammer into the zawn, and she herself climbed down and rescued them from the sea.

For that first performance of *The Tempest* there was no stage lighting as such. Batteries and car headlights, weak power brought down from Minack House, and an obliging moon supplied all the lighting that there was. There was no permanent stage set, no balustrade, no wire netting, no concrete, car park, box office, archways, dressing-rooms, or any of the amenities that are there now. The box office was a table at the edge of the lawn near the house, and everyone went down the steep, narrow path between furze bushes to get to the theatre. When *The Times* printed a long column about the performance of *The Tempest* in this idyllic setting, public interest in the theatre spread beyond the Tamar, and ultimate fame was inevitable. The following year *Twelfth Night* was chosen, the nucleus of players had firmly established themselves, and their ranks were augmented by two professional actors, Stephen Jack of the Liverpool Repertory Company, who played Orsino, and Neil Porter then of the Old Vic, who played Antonio, the sea captain.

Already the theatre was beginning to grow. Audiences at the first production had expressed alarm at the, apparently, straight drop into the sea in which a wrong move or an inadvertent step backwards might land any one of the actors. To allay their fears a balustrade and some small pillars were added and, with the addition of large shrubs apparently growing on the stage, it assumed the appearance of a formal garden, and was as perfect a setting for *Twelfth Night* as it had been for *The Tempest*. This was an Illyria we shall never see again, alas.

The year 1935 had a triple bill, and further additions to the theatre, with larger pillars on the stage, a throne, and the dais on which it stood, and which is still there. By 1937, patrons, publicity, and press were firmly established and it seemed that the Minack Open-Air Theatre was equally firmly established as a summer attraction for the inhabitants of Cornwall and any visitors who came to its shores, and in those days Cornwall was not the tourist centre it has now become. That year, Neil Porter, who had played in *Twelfth Night,* was responsible for the most ambitious production this theatre had yet seen—Shakespeare's *Antony and Cleopatra.* It is interesting to note that the magnificent costumes and properties for all these early plays were designed and made by Hilda Quick and Rowena Cade. The memory of individual performances fades, but who, having seen the beautiful décor for that production of *Antony and Cleopatra,* could forget the impact on the beholder, especially in conjunction with a moon like a great copper plate shining over the sea and the scene.

I remember on a blue and golden afternoon in the summer of 1939 sitting in the theatre with a very young friend to watch the first professional company of actors under the aegis of Violet Vanbrugh and Walter Berssenbrugge play an adaptation of *The Count of Monte Cristo,* which they alternated with Masefield's *Tristan and Isolt*; and how impossible it seemed then that war was imminent. The unruffled sea dreamed below the theatre, the sun shone warm on actors and audience, and gulls on translucent wings wheeled overhead. Little of the play made any lasting impression on me, but I shall never forget the beauty and peace of that lazy afternoon, in direct dramatic contrast to the feeling of foreboding that the world would be plunged into war for the second time in a life.

During the war, the Minack as a theatre ceased to exist. Barbed wire was everywhere and an anti-aircraft gun post, now the box office, was built at the top of the cliff. Miss Cade managed to keep the stage grass cut, by crawling under the wire with the mowing machine, but she must have wondered if the players would ever strut and fret their hour upon her stage again. Scenes from a film starring Stewart Grainger and Margaret Lockwood were shot in the theatre in 1944, but having taken a dummy grand piano down the cliff, and erected three stucco columns (which blew down in a gale), the film people decided to remove themselves and their gear, and build another papier

The grass stage presents real difficulties for a ballet production but the
Ballets Minerva company improvise with a tarpaulin

Cambridge University Players' 1964 production of Shakespeare's *The Winter's Tale*

The first production at the Minack, Shakespeare's *The Tempest* 1932

mâché Minack in the Gainsborough studios. When they left
they had removed the small pillars built for *Antony and Cleopatra* and the remains of the balustrade not already destroyed
by the Army; the Italian prisoners of war who took down the
barbed wire entanglements knocked the big throne into the sea,
and the theatre must have looked as bare as it did for the first
production. Surely few people would have had the heart to start
all over again, but by 1949 Miss Cade and Billy Rawlings had
built another balustrade, another large throne and more 'broken'
pillars, and at the end of July the Minack Theatre reopened
with a perfect play for that most lovely setting, Euripides' *The
Trojan Women*. It was produced by Miss G. M. Tranter with
pupils of the Penzance County Grammar Schools, and over a
span of nearly twenty years remains in the memory as one of the
most beautiful performances staged in this theatre. I think I am
right in saying that the girl who played Andromache was the
first of the Minack amateurs to turn professional, and is well
known now as Avril Elgar.

Then came the Festival of Britain in 1957. Nobody really
knew what the festival was about, but we were told to enjoy
ourselves, and enjoy ourselves we did. Or at least, some of us
did. But in the interim between *The Trojan Women* and the
festival many changes had taken place at the Minack. At this
time Cornwall had as its country drama adviser the dynamic
Frances Collingwood Selby, and it was originally her idea that
the Festival of Britain should be celebrated in Cornwall by a
festival of amateur drama. Up and down the county new plays
were written and old Cornish tales and history re-told in
dramatic form, with such a wealth of good things to see that it
was impossible to visit them all.

With the reopening of the theatre after the war, Miss Cade
felt that help both in funds and labour would be needed to run
it. She and the faithful Billy were still active, but they were ten
years older. With a view to getting a public body to take over
the theatre and its management they began the immense task of
putting a boundary fence round it to cut it out of the Minack

House garden and give it a separate approach road. One of the big London drama schools and the National Trust were both interested in the proposition, but at the time neither could afford even part of the cost of the fencing. However, a county organisation, the Cornwall branch of the National Council of Social Services, became interested and in due course Miss Cade handed the theatre over to it, understanding that no difficulty would be met in carrying out her plans for the necessities of a working theatre: lighting, dressing-rooms, cloakrooms, comfortable seating and, first of all, an approach road with right of access for theatre traffic over a quarter of a mile of privately-owned land. This right of approach was never obtained during the council's three years of administration and, in the February of 1955, it said it had made a considerable loss on the theatre and was no longer interested in running it.

In the meantime the old firm of Cade and Rawlings pressed steadily on with the work. They knocked down 200 yd of drystone wall (or Cornish 'hedge') and rebuilt it farther back in the house garden, to make a 30-ft carriageway to the theatre car park on top of the cliff. When you visit the theatre and look at the size of the stones in the wall that runs from the theatre gate to the car park, you get some idea of the immensity of the task involved. Between them, Miss Cade and Billy made fence posts and erected fencing, and during the council's tenure, at its request made a path from Porthcurno beach up to the box office, a feat which necessitated making 90 steps in the cliff. They also carried out major alterations to the stage itself to suit the requirements of the festival play.

The popularity of Cornwall as a holiday centre was rapidly growing, and the Festival of Britain was destined to put the Minack Theatre firmly on the map. Mrs Nora Ratcliff, the well-known lecturer and dramatist, was commissioned to write a play expressly for the Minack, with a thoroughly Cornish theme and a team of Cornish actors, and the subject of her choice was the Tristan legend. For this the broken pillars and graceful balustrade were considered unsuitable, and the finale of Mrs

Ratcliffe's play, *Tristan of Cornwall*, required a solid structure on which the bodies of the ill-fated lovers could rest. The pseudo-Greek appearance of the stage was transformed into the pseudo-Celtic blocks that stand there today, and the table, which has in its time played many parts since then, and is affectionately known to actors and directors as the Mousetrap or the Fish-slab, was originally built to bear the bodies on their biers. Financially it was impossible to use dressed granite, which would have been the ideal material for the new and permanent set, but Miss Cade added decorative carvings to the concrete to mitigate the starkness, and at least those who never saw the original stage will never mourn its beauty, lost for ever.

Tristan of Cornwall, although it was the only play to be presented at the theatre in 1951, was the forerunner of what has become an established summer season of amateur drama, with groups from all over the United Kingdom clamouring for 'a week at the Minack'. Those early post-war productions were splendidly dressed by Miss Marjorie Ballance, of St Ives, whose professional knowledge of stage design did so much to fill the Minack with glowing colour and flowing costume and who was responsible for the very high standard set by the Cornish groups for the costuming of all their plays. *Tristan of Cornwall* received wide acclamation, not only from the local press but in the national papers and illustrated weeklies as well. The company of players eventually became the West Cornwall Theatre Group, which existed solely for the benefit of the Minack, the profits from their productions being ploughed back into the theatre, and it is mainly due to them that the Minack survived its brief spell of public ownership. This same group's highly successful production of *Macbeth* in 1955 provided the present backstage dressing-room. Before this was built, dressing for the plays presented serious problems for the players! The Council of Social Services provided a 30-ft marquee, and to erect it Miss Cade and Billy had first to level another terrace beyond the gully and overlooking Porthcurno Bay. It was hoped that eventually this second terrace could be turned into a covered theatre for use in wet weather, but up to the present this has not proved practicable. However, the marquee duly arrived and was erected. But the shelf on which it stood is a draughty spot and, as any camper knows, guy ropes need constant attention— and Cornish weather is variable and unpredictable. When the cast of *Everyman* arrived one evening, it was to find the marquee flat, on top of all their costumes and make-up, and 30 ft of canvas weighs a considerable amount. Marjorie Ballance, who made all the costumes for the production, organised the rescue squad and the play opened on time and with due calm and dignity; but perhaps it was just as well that the second terrace is out of earshot of the auditorium! After this unfortunate attempt at a covered dressing place, Miss Cade gave the actors the run of Minack House, and one year they used the small bungalow on the left of the approach lane—a long way from the stage if by mischance some vital garment or property was forgotten.

It was the West Cornwall Theatre Group which was responsible for introducing the 'midnight matinée', that mixed blessing so dearly beloved of the stage electricians, but not always so popular with the older members of casts. At its inception it was an immensely popular gimmick, so much so that nobody foresaw the utter chaos that ensued when the cars coming away from the ordinary evening performance met the cars coming up for the midnight matinée. On one occasion a coach party and the bus got locked together on one of the narrow bends of the old road, since considerably widened and ironed out, and neither coach nor bus could budge, either forwards or back. People intending to see the play at the Minack parked their cars in a field and walked the whole length of the valley, up Maunsell's hill, and down to the theatre, a distance of at least a mile and a half. I believe that part of a hedge had to be removed before the bus and coach could part company. Another time, a local farmer came to the rescue and directed the outgoing cars across a series of bumpy fields, to meet the Porthcurno road higher up the valley above the Cables and Wireless buildings.

Now it is is usual to have an afternoon performance if there is to be a 'midnight', but attendances at the latter are not as overwhelming since the novelty wore off, and many companies no longer play them.

In 1953 there were three separate productions by Cornish groups, with two plays specially written for the Minack and Nicholson's *Prophesy to the Wind*, produced by Frances Collingwood Selby, with a most moving and beautiful performance by Nesta Cuddeford, who in 1961 was such an outstanding Queen Elizabeth in Schiller's *Mary Stuart*. Ardingly College Drama Club paid the first of several visits under the leadership of Richard Hamilton, and so the number of plays in the summer increased and by 1954 the season was an established fact.

Another professional company, the Ballets Minerva, braved the hazards of rocks and rough paths in tutus and blocked shoes, and danced on a large tarpaulin stretched across the stage in front of 'the circle'—thistledown blown on the sea wind! And in 1956 an attempt was made to stage Inglis Gundry's opera *The Logan Rock*, but open-air opera was not altogether successful, as the merest suspicion of sea mist or drizzle caused the strings in the orchestra to fly for shelter for their instruments, bringing the performance to an abrupt conclusion. This opera, for which fine weather was so essential, held the all-time bad luck record, being able to play only three out of eleven scheduled performances.

It is a fact that people often come to the theatre to sit on the cliffs on a summer evening and revel in the unique setting or perhaps each other's company, but when daylight fades and the backcloth is a velvet darkness, then the electricians in the lighting box take over and, though the bats and moths dart across the stage, a different spell succeeds the magic of the sunset glow on the Logan Rock: the inexplicable, wholly enchanting magic of 'theatre' pure and simple; and whether it be the Minack, or Epidaurus, or the Regent's Park Theatre in London, the play's the thing. Then the director and his lighting expert come into their own and take possession of the stage from their eyrie above the auditorium, the weatherproof, warm, commanding structure

23

now known as the Lighthouse, far removed from the days when the lanterns were precariously balanced among the rocks and each one had to be guarded by an attendant spirit to see that it was not blown over, knocked over, or otherwise damaged. Only the switchboard and record player were in a sort of tarpaulin tent, the mooring hooks for which are still there, behind the present Lighthouse. Ten years ago Fry's *Boy with a Cart* was performed without any lighting at all, the only stage effect being a temperamental Calor gas flood placed at the top of the steps on stage right, to shine on Cuthman as he led his villagers up to their completed church, the last moment of the play. For this production the large throne that replaced the one the Italians knocked into the zawn had to be disguised as the village well, since a throne had no place in the very simple story. In 1958 Miss Cade removed the throne altogether, leaving the beautiful little dais acting area free for whatever demands producers made on it. This second throne was broken up and used in the construction of the steps leading up from the pool at the bottom of the slope, offstage left.

Not until the 60s was there an adequate lighting box, though a temporary affair was built on what is now called the Royal Box. Even with the electricity laid on by the South Western Electricity Board, and enough equipment to satisfy the needs of most amateur stage electricians, there are always unexpected excitements and unrehearsed effects during a season. *The Lady's Not For Burning* nearly burnt out the old box in 1960, and in 1965 the Cambridge University Players' *Lear* was plunged in total darkness and is described elsewhere in these pages.

In the old days there was no lighting below the stage, and only a couple of strands of wire between the actors awaiting their cues and the sea in the zawn below. For one funeral procession, the corpse-bearers had to insist on a hurricane lantern at the lower steps from the slope down to behind the stage, in case the whole cortège disappeared into the sea. And to reach the far side of the stage from the dressing-room entailed a steep and hazardous climb up the cliff behind the gully, across the programme-and-cushion terrace to the stairs leading down to stage left. And these were not the only hazards of putting on a play at the Minack.

For the Cornwall Religious Drama Fellowship's production of Fry's *The Firstborn*, a sphynx was made by two members of the group during the winter months, and when the time came, it was carried down the cliffs in a howling gale and anchored with ropes and wires across the concrete table on the stage. During the week's run of the play it was found necessary to keep a pot of grey paint under the table to paint out the scores of autographs scribbled over it by visitors to the theatre in the daytime, and at the end of the week after a night of pouring rain there was so little of it left that the remains were thrown into the zawn—the end of months of patient labour.

When the Fellowship produced *The Marvellous History of St Bernard*, another papier mâché figure was made by the same two members who had fashioned the well round the throne, and the ill-fated sphynx. The statue of the Devil, an integral part of the story, was mounted on the wall dividing the theatre from the Minack House garden, but when the time came for its removal, it was discovered that a swarm of bees had taken up residence inside it during the run of the play. The local police were contacted, and they found a bee-keeper who removed most of the swarm; but the producer, who was also stage manager and 'transport' and had the task of removing the statue and the rest of the stage properties in an ancient Hillman brake, can tell a painful story of those that remained! It was for this production that Miss Cade and Billy enlarged a narrow crack in the rocks above stage right, to give easy and dignified access to the small ledge that has since served so many other useful purposes. The producer, thoughtfully pondering on problems presented by the play, thoughtlessly said to Miss Cade, 'I do wish that crack was big enough for Heaven, then we could have the Devil on the mountain far left, and Heaven taking a benign interest in the world below, up right.' And lo, before the next season, the crack *was* big enough for as much of Heaven as

25

was necessary to the play. That is what it is like to work at the Minack.

Only once has *Hamlet* been staged in this theatre, in 1962 by the West Cornwall Theatre Group under the direction of John Bryant, and with costumes by Gwladys Main of St Buryan, whose gorgeous garments have since been such a feature of the group's productions; the following week the Playgoers' Theatre Club of Penzance put on the first play for children, Nicholas Stuart Grey's *Beauty and the Beast*. For *Hamlet* it was essential that the Ghost should be able to appear unexpectedly in different parts of the theatre, and to enable it to do this, Miss Cade built steps behind the 'heaven' she had already made for St Bernard. To allow Beauty's father, Mr Clement, to be blown through the gates of the Beast's castle and land below the stage in comparative safety, she collected driftwood from the beach and rocks, and made a staircase leading down from the circle which is still in use today. Later, there were two productions of *Toad of Toad Hall*, one by the Fletcher Players of Cambridge and the following year by the Leicester Drama Society. The Fletcher Players, who are now among 'the regulars', are the only group that brings its own musicians with it, and has 'live' music for its plays. The University and Christ Church Dramatic Societies brought a very sophisticated *Alice in Wonderland*, but as yet there have been few plays at the theatre specifically intended for the young in heart of all ages.

With the ever-increasing numbers of theatre viewers throughout the year, it became more and more difficult to keep the greensward of the stage; turfing, sowing, wire netting laid over the whole area, requests to the public to keep off the grass all proved unavailing, and by 1964, except for a thin layer on the 'circle', there was no stage grass left, and no chance of growing any more. That was a good year for weather, but not so good for the bone-dry stage. In the West Cornwall Theatre Group's production of *Twelfth Night*, Andrew Aguecheek skidded on the loose gravel and broke his knee-cap, and his part had to be taken over by the producer, John Bryant. Three weeks later the

Penzance Playgoers' Club kicked up so much dust with the final dance of their production of *Much Ado About Nothing* that the first few rows of the audience were choked and blinded to such an extent that Miss Cade abandoned all hope of another grass stage, and instead she paved the whole expanse with the exception of the 'circle' in softly coloured, different-sized hexagonal tiles. This further labour of Hercules she achieved during the winter months, herself filling sacks with sand for the concrete from Porthcurno beach, and carrying them down the cliff to the theatre one at a time. While she worked on the stage, she levelled the rake by at least 4 in, so that the actors no longer have a sharp uphill walk from the balustrade to the prompt box. Over the years she has replaced the uncomfortable wooden seats, which were used in the construction of the first lighting box, with the deep, comfortable 'stalls' of today; the gully, that favourite viewing point of so many of the regulars, is banked with concrete tiers of seats, steps have been made on either side of the Lighthouse, and each concrete seat has been carved with the title and date of a different production at the theatre. Inevitably there have been repetitions, always interesting though not always felicitous, and in every season there has been at least one exciting production, some beautiful ones, and occasionally an extremely odd one.

The hard little slatted chairs that accommodated the first audiences disappeared after the war, and the Council for Social Services installed some equally hard wooden school benches for the first row of the audience. These were the ones that were broken up and used to make the first lighting box to house what little equipment the theatre had; but it was not until 1966 that the present Lighthouse was built above the first box, to house the considerable installation that the theatre owns today.

Only recently has the path below the stage been securely fenced, and a small dressing-room known as The Cabin has been built under the rocks to the right of the auditorium, a godsend for the actors, who had to effect any quick change of costume in the dark at the bottom of the slope, where there is a

pool into which one actor at least has inadvertently stepped—
probably more, if history related each occurrence! At one time,
players were allowed to use the cliff garden belonging to the
house as a green room, and the gateways were built above and
below the theatre to give them access to the garden and were
kept locked when not in use, but it is a shaming thought that
some of the companies who played at the Minack left so much
litter in the garden that eventually the privilege was withdrawn.
And litter is one of the theatre's great problems which Miss
Cade, in her quiet, self-effacing way deals with herself after
every performance.

At one time the eruption of the audience on to the stage was
another problem peculiar to the theatre, but a note in every
programme requesting the audience to keep off the stage has at
last achieved the desired result. Never shall I forget a matinée
when an entire girls' school swarmed down on to the stage and
even started up the steps leading to the dressing-room the
moment the interval was announced, and the rapid action taken
by an unknown member of the audience who rose up and roared
to them to return to their seats in a voice that brought them all
scuttling back off the stage as fast as they could make it. Having
myself acted once or twice at the Minack, and produced plays
on that stage, I can say with feeling how much the players
appreciate the tacit recognition of that 'fourth wall' that divides
them from the audience, and helps to retain the illusion that is
so much a part of any theatre; but although audiences now
respect the actor's privacy offstage, the same cannot always be
said of the casual visitors who have been known to climb up
from the rocks below and arrive on stage in the middle of a performance. It is by no means unusual, despite the fact that it
must be perfectly obvious to the smallest intelligence that a play
is being performed; but on occasion, a furious stage manager or
stage hand has had to make a dash for the intruders and get
rid of them—quick! To prevent further unwelcome sightseers
from Minack Rock, Miss Cade has had to build another gate
below the theatre; and has also had to build out an extension to

the box office to ensure a one-way only passage past the office for performances. 'Tis pity that 'tis true.

From the early beginnings with one or possibly two plays in the summer, the season now extends for eleven weeks, from the middle of June till the beginning of September, and belongs, with very few exceptions, to the amateurs. In 1967 attendances for the season were 21,685. Normally the theatre holds about 450, but the record for any one performance was for the Cambridge University Players' production of Robert Bolt's *A Man for All Seasons* when, somehow or other, the cliff accommodated 806 people, far too many for anyone's comfort, except perhaps the actors' and the box office. One of the difficulties facing the theatre management is the fact that it is nine miles from anywhere, and people who come long distances to see a play, often prefer to see it uncomfortably rather than go home without seeing it at all, and it is very hard to turn enthusiastic latecomers away. But a system has now been evolved by which the box office people know when all the seats are taken, and a limited number of 'standing room only' places, at half price, are allowed in.

The last war, which closed the theatre and threatened its very existence, was indirectly responsible for its present management. As a boy, Tony Soper was evacuated with his school from Plymouth to Penzance, falling in love with Cornwall in general and the far west in particular. In recent years, through a mutual friend, he met Miss Cade and promptly succumbed to the spell of the Minack. He became interested in the problems of the theatre, the running of which grew more and more complicated as its popularity spread far and wide among amateur drama groups aspiring to play there; and increasingly difficult to run. In 1964 he agreed to manage the theatre for one year in order to help it over a difficult period. The one year lengthened to two and inevitably to three and four, and at the time of writing he is still firmly billed on the posters as manager, although he still insists that he knows less than anyone about theatres or plays!

In the choice of play for the Minack I suppose there will

always be a certain amount of controversy as to what is 'good Minack'. Most of the productions here are good, nearly all enjoyable, and there have been some which were outstanding in every way. Some productions have been lifted straight from a society's own 'little theatre' and put down on the Minack stage, furniture, properties and all, some successfully, others less happily; and there have been productions with only the stage as it stands, a minimum of properties, and the imagination of the audience to 'piece out the imperfections with its thoughts'. It is not my place to discuss in these pages the choice of play or the manner of presentation, but having seen all but twenty-three of the theatre's 110 productions, I would venture the opinion that, on the whole, the most successful ones are those that leave the theatre to itself and the stage as uncluttered as possible. Miss Cade has provided the bare essentials, and many and varied are the uses to which they can be put. The table that bore the bodies of Tristan and Isolt has been Malvolio's prison, the altar of Artemis in Tauris, the golden throne of Alexander the Great, Juliet's balcony, even the tomb of Thomas á Becket, who, with stoic fortitude, lay on it like a marble effigy until the last of the audience had left the theatre. The grass circle, the crack in the rocks at the bottom of the steps on stage right, the prompt box, the steps down to the stage on the far left, the pillars, the 'stone' seats, the dais, the rock built into the stage itself, the openings under the front stalls for extra lighting—used with such dramatic effect by The Interluders of Hertford in their production of *Peer Gynt*—everything on the stage at the Minack proclaims the imagination, patience, skill, and innate sense of theatre of the woman whose life work it is.

Everything possible has been done, or will be done, for the comfort and convenience of actors and audiences. People often ask if the theatre is dangerous, or the descent to it difficult. Years ago an elderly lady missed her footing at the top of the path and slithered down the grass bank to be 'fielded' by Miss Cade and a friend, and a conveniently situated gorse bush. A stout wooden fence was erected to prevent any further mishaps of a like nature. The cliff path has now been doubled in width, the zigzags are on a fairly easy gradient with lighting at all the turns and, with ropes to hold alongside the path, even the most timid need have no fear of the climb, up or down. Occasionally there has been an accident which might well happen in any other theatre, but always preventive measures were taken to avoid as far as possible any repetition of the mishap, either in the auditorium or on the stage; and if any visitor to the theatre exercises due care and commonsense, nothing untoward is likely to happen. Anyone with a weak heart or suffering from vertigo can survey the theatre in safety behind that stout wooden railing at the top of the path, and having scanned the distance and the slope, can judge if either is likely to present too much of a hazard.

As for the actors, directors, technicians, backstage crew, and even authors, the theatre can be cruel to them, or it can be infinitely rewarding. The whole level of amateur acting and production, in the best sense of the word 'amateur', has reached a standard all over the country that would make those early productions at the Minack, and in countless village halls and town pavilions, seem amateur indeed. The gap between the amateur and professional stage has narrowed; amateurs, in what little spare time they have after their ordinary day's work, dedicate so much of themselves in so many ways to the art of the theatre, to drama, costume, lighting, all that goes into the making of a play for the delectation of an audience, and the satisfaction of that strange urge which demands a lighted stage for its fulfilment—'that one talent which is death to hide'—and one and all we fall victims to this particular siren, this Minack Theatre at Porthcurno near Land's End. And for Rowena Cade, to whom this unique and magical theatre owes its being, we who in one way or another have been intimately concerned with it over the years have compiled this book; we offer it to her and to her public, with gratitude for her labour of love which has given so much delight to so many people and with our own personal and deep affection for herself.

CHAPTER 2

Directing at the Minack

FRANK BECHHOFER

Every year since 1960 I have directed a play at the Minack
Theatre. This simple statement conceals a great deal. It
implies that the Minack has somehow become part of a
way of life, not only for me, but now for my family and many of
my closest friends. There must be something special about the
Minack. After all a director can work on plays in his home
town, in a local theatre; there is no need to travel 600 miles or
more as I do from Edinburgh to the south-western edge of
England, in order to direct a play. And if we include the complications of running a company gathered from the ends of the
earth, even if there is always a nucleus in Cambridge, collecting
together the necessary equipment and taking some three weeks
of holiday to do the job, then I am sure you will agree that there
is something very special about the Minack. In this chapter I
am going to try and give some idea of the particular problems
and pleasures involved in directing a play there. Inevitably we
shall touch on other aspects of the task, be they lighting, 'prop'
design, or acting, since in a way the director is concerned with
them all. But the main focus will be on the process of creating a
stage play from the raw material of script, actors, technicians
and equipment.

In the evening after our final matinée, just before leaving the
theatre for the last time that season, I like to stand at the top of
the auditorium, more or less at that point where the stage first

32

comes into full view, and think back over the events of the previous seventeen days. We are one of the very few companies
fortunate enough to be able to arrange our affairs so that we can
rehearse from start to finish down in Cornwall and contain the
production proper within the space of those crowded few days.
If I am lucky the last touches of the evening sun will be on the
upper reaches of the auditorium and the stage will be in light
shadow. It is in a way the memory of that last moment, when
the play as produced has disappeared for the last time, that
draws me back to the Minack again and again. For it is in the
nature of most of the live theatre, one of its most attractive and
saddening features, that a play lives its brief life anew from the
start of the action to the end of each performance, finally dying
at the end of the run never to reappear again in the same form.
Standing on the cliff path then in the silence of the evening I remember the growth of that particular play, the rehearsals, the
companionship of the other members of the company both in
the theatre and in the evenings, the tenseness and excitement of
the first moments of the first performance, the parts I feel I
handled well, and of course, the parts I feel I could and should
have handled better. But now the stage is silent for a few hours
until the next company arrives to people it again with characters,
those strange creatures half-way between reality and illusion.
And I think it is at that moment that the urge to start again, to
do another play, better if possible, comes over me and the
definite decision to do it again, which was never really in doubt,
is taken. For no director can look at a silent theatre as beautiful
and challenging as the Minack without wanting to fill it with
actors, audience and above all a play.

The story of the play which has just ended started long before
the beginning of rehearsals. It was chosen some seven or eight
months before, and this question of choosing a play is the first
problem the Minack sets the director. All theatres are more
suitable for one kind of play rather than another but the Minack
places stronger constraints on the range of choice than most.
Paradoxically, one *could*, I think, do any play that had no over-

whelming technical complications on the Minack stage. I suspect it is possible to 'get away with' more or less all styles and periods of play, to do them tolerably well and hold the audience. But I believe that to treat the Minack just like any other stage is a mistake. By careful choice it is possible to get the theatre on your side, to get it working for you. The stage is very broad if not particularly deep and can give the impression of great spaciousness. It is obviously throwing away an advantage to do a play that is tightly enclosed, claustrophobic or demands a small fixed stage area. Yet on the other hand, at night the theatre is perhaps at its most effective when only a portion of the stage is lit, and the rest shades off into darkness. Thus a play which gives an opportunity for breaking the stage up into areas and not using all of it throughout can be a good choice.

At first glance it would seem that a play having a largely outdoor setting is called for, and certainly it is easy to create an outdoor impression! Yet curiously the layout of the stage, with its formal pillars left of centre, its stone floor and huge 'table' more or less at the centre back, lends itself to indoor scenes, at least of a formal kind. It is perhaps easier to create the feeling of a palace, courtroom, or dungeon, than that of the Forest of Arden . . . there is a distinct shortage of trees on the theatre! The presence of the sea is always useful of course, particularly in Shakespeare who had a distinct tendency to work sea scenes into his plays either centrally or peripherally. But I have myself come to the conclusion that if the playwright's words are good enough the Minack's basic stage setting is sufficiently neutral to lend itself to most scenes. Most scenes yes, but not by any means most stage settings. There are many difficulties confronting any company which lets itself in for a great deal of scene changing on the Minack. Everything has to be done in full view and quick scene changes are even more necessary than they are in the indoor theatre. But the Minack obviously does not possess a grid for hanging scenery, a revolve, or the other aids to scene changing in the indoor theatre. More or less everything has to be done by human labour without the aid of machinery,

This picture was taken in the days when the stage was still grass and the lighting box was an old shed

The West Cornwall Theatre Group's 1955 production of Shakespeare's *Macbeth*

and this coupled with the size of the stage puts the emphasis on quick, simple scene changes with the minimum of furniture or setting. I shall have some more to say about this question of setting later, but for the moment it is enough to point out that it affects the choice of play.

Sitting in the auditorium of the theatre, the audience is looking at a natural setting of great beauty and colour. It is also a somewhat unnatural setting, in which actors dressed in the clothes of today somehow look slightly 'wrong'. Modern plays set in the present day have been done most successfully at the Minack, but I have a personal preference either for costume plays or at any rate plays which can be colourfully dressed. A cast full of characters in lounge suits and discreet dresses would find it hard to make the maximum impact on this stage.

The final feature which affects the choice of play is once again the size of the Minack, coupled now with the vagaries of the Cornish weather. Plays performed there have to be both windproof and rainproof! There are times when very intimate scenes are almost impossible because of the necessity of being heard above the wind and rain. And, anyway, intimacy is not an easy feeling to create when the water is pouring down the actor's back and his hair is plastered over his eyes. Now this is not to be taken as meaning that intimate scenes cannot be played at the Minack, or that they are to be shunned like the plague. Far from it, but it does imply that plays depending largely on such scenes are perhaps best avoided. In contrast the stage is wonderfully suited for some things: Shakespearian battles, Greek plays, large outdoor scenes, most formal settings, and plays with a strong rhetorical content. Yet, paradoxically again, too much rhetoric seems false on this curious stage with its strange blend of size, formality and intimacy. For there is a sense in which the theatre is an intimate one. Because the playing area has very little depth the actor is close to his audience, at any rate the lower part of it, and plays requiring a high degree of actor/audience contact are well suited to the stage. The soliloquy—at least the type given to the audience—can be very successfully handled.

Directing at the Minack

When choosing a play for this theatre the director somehow has to balance these various factors one against another. Every reader will be able to think of favourite plays which he would like to see in this marvellous setting, and also, no doubt, of others which he reluctantly has to admit are unsuitable or impracticable. In the last resort, however, it is perhaps worth remembering that most plays *can* be done on the Minack and there is one other factor of overwhelming importance, at least in the amateur theatre. Companies have to do plays which they can cast! The actor is after all the director's chief tool, weapon and asset. Without good actors there is a very definite limit to what can be done. With good actors, in the right parts, many difficulties can be overcome. In the end, when rehearsals are over and the play starts for the first time, everything depends on the actor. In rehearsal the director should have established the shape, the pace, the style of the play. And he should also, if he has a good working relationship with his actors, have improved, moulded and changed their performances. But with the opening night the director's task is done and all rests with the actor. No play however well directed can succeed without good acting; many a play has been at least partially saved by really good acting from the effects of mediocre direction. As a company we generally decide on a play which we think will suit the theatre but only make the final decision when we know we can cast it.

Choosing an actor to play a part at the Minack is the same as choosing an actor to work anywhere, with a few additional complications! There are a few bonuses as well of course. A rather unusual one is that the angle of the auditorium makes it difficult to judge height; as a result it may be possible to put up with disparities in the height of actors which would not be admissible on conventional stages. On the Minack the actor faces vocal difficulties which are seldom presented to the amateur. One requires actors with better voice and breath control than average. To be successful in this theatre an actor must be able to produce and project his voice properly, and I personally give this great weight during casting. As one listens to actors auditioning, generally in a fairly small room on a bleak day in February, one has mentally to transfer them to the Minack stage. Not only must the voice be an interesting, flexible one; somehow one has to assess how well it will carry, which is largely a matter of timbre and clarity; also how powerful it is, which is largely a matter of breath control and natural physique. One has to imagine the actor both on a hot, windstill, sun-drenched stage in mid-afternoon and also on that same stage on a wild, stormy night with the wind howling and often rain pelting down as well. And the necessity to have actors who will perform under these conditions as well as rehearse very intensively for ten days, while living communally as we do in somewhat primitive temporary quarters, means that the director has to consider personal qualities which do not normally figure very large in allocating parts. For a man who can cope with a smallish part under these circumstances may apparently have the technical and artistic ability for a far larger part but possess neither the physique, stamina nor personality to carry it off at the Minack.

Because of the nature of the stage one requires actors who can give neat, clear performances. The actor who works largely by minute changes of facial expression, no matter how successful he may be in a small club theatre, will not succeed at this one. Movement, of course, matters in any theatre. But in very few theatres does the actor have a chance of travelling for 70 ft from left to right! To run naturally across the Minack stage, particularly when wearing tights, is something many find an ordeal and some simply cannot do. To walk across it slowly, which at times can be stunningly effective, is far from easy. So any actor who is to have a large part must be able to move competently and confidently. Stillness is a great asset in any actor but on this vast stage it is a powerful weapon. Small movements tend either to look fussy here or to be totally ineffectual. The most effective actors on the Minack as regards movement and gesture are the ones who contrast clearly a state of stillness and a strong move or gesture. Of course this is true of all actors everywhere, but the Minack stage seems to be particularly hard on an actor's technique. Actors who are quite competent, if not very exciting, on a small indoor stage often show up very badly, appearing either 'flat' or 'hammy'. I can only hazard a guess why this is so, but I would put a lot of it down to the fact that the Minack itself is not only a very natural setting but is at the same time in a way 'larger than life-size'. As a result of the technical ability of the actor to give a performance which is both 'naturalistic' but larger than life is stretched to the limit. It follows, of course, that actors tend to improve as they get more used to the stage and previous Minack experience counts for a good deal.

When casting for this theatre a final consideration is that of physical strain. To play a big part here requires an actor who is physically fit and has a lot of stamina. And it follows from this that an actor playing a long lead needs support, good support, even more desperately than the same actor playing indoors under normal conditions. I have always been of the opinion that to pin a play on one lead actor is bad policy at all times. On the Minack I believe it to be short-sighted in the extreme. It is for this reason that I have always aimed at achieving an integrated effect. I am sure that a director casting for the Minack should go for all-round strength rather than a single outstanding performance. This is a problem frequently encountered in the amateur theatre. Given certain actors as available one often finds that if the lead (say) is cast ideally the two main supporting parts are anything but ideal, whereas shuffling all three will produce a less outstanding lead but all-round strength. I would have no doubt at all which to go for in this particular theatre. To carry a play there virtually on one's own would be a tremendous strain. Deliberately choosing to place an actor under such a strain would be a very dangerous path for a director to follow.

Now we have chosen our play and managed to get it cast so that barring illnesses and accidents we shall go into rehearsal with suitable actors. Between casting and the start of rehearsals a lot has to be done in the production of any play. I am con-

cerned here with the particular problems the Minack poses, not
with the general task of directing a play, but this theatre tends to
create its own problems in almost every quarter! I shall not,
however, discuss the detailed preparation which the director
must go through before rehearsal begins. At this stage everyone
works in a different way. Certainly decisions must be taken,
even if only preliminary ones, about setting, costumes, properties, lighting and music. How far this preparation goes will
depend on the way in which the particular director and his
company work, and on such things as the technical facilities
available. Personally I like to have the set and furniture decided
completely before we go to Cornwall. Building can take place
there, as I like the setting to be very simple. Costumes have to be
considered well in advance, especially if they are to be designed
and made specially for the production. A good deal of extra
lighting equipment has to be chosen and taken down to Cornwall. I like to have the music completely fixed and recorded
before rehearsal begins. But what sort of *special* problems does
the Minack pose? First of all let us think again about this
question of setting.

The great difficulty is that the entire theatre is so large, so
solid and so unified. As a result I have come to the conclusion
that it is no use trying to compete with solid concrete! Stage sets
are generally made of combinations of wood, canvas, hardboard, polystyrene and so on and they just don't look like concrete. It is very difficult to make sets which blend into the stage.
The Minack stage is in a sense already a set. And this is the in-
superable difficulty. No matter what you put on the stage it
doesn't look as though it is part of the permanent setting unless
it is made of concrete. Even ordinary rostra tend to look false.
Furniture, on the other hand, is all right, as one expects furniture to have a different appearance and texture from the room
in which it is found. I have twice put gates across the pillars
(left centre) and this has been a success I think. This is probably
because one does not expect gates to look like walls for instance.
But I once put a vast box-like construction across between the

pillars, purely because I couldn't think of a better way around the problem of bringing Hermione on as a statue in *The Winter's Tale*. The box was, of course, equipped with an opening at the back as well as the front, and she could get in from behind out of view of the audience. It didn't really work, although we solved the problem of bringing it on quickly and smoothly and it did not disrupt the action to any extent. But it just looked wrong. Try as we did to blend it in to the surroundings, wood and hardboard didn't look like concrete. This was especially so during matinées. As a matter of fact it did look quite reasonable at night, but in the daytime it was something of a failure. I still cannot think of a better way of doing it, however, given that I wanted her centre stage, and it just points the fact that sometimes one may have to put up with machinery. But if it can possibly be avoided I would never use it. The combination of the naturalness of the setting and the somewhat difficult building material chosen makes me certain that ordinary sets should be shunned. This does not apply, of course, to small items such as sign boards (inn-signs say), small screens and so on. Anything, in fact, which does not pretend to look like the rest of the set can be used. The basic fact which has to be grasped is that the Minack is not like an empty indoor stage. It is an already set stage and any further setting has to take this into account. The designer does not start with a neutral area.

Although furniture at any rate looks perfectly all right there are, of course, limits. It is probably best to keep the amount down to a minimum, both because it is difficult to move on and off and because too much would begin to conflict with its surroundings. A realistic interior would be both impossible and absurd. For the same reason solid plain furniture looks better than elaborate pieces. To some extent, as I said before, this affects the choice of play. Valuable furniture cannot be used because it may well get soaked and this generally means making pieces specially. Designers and carpenters are warned that this has its own problems. A rather attractive line in stools with curved seats was made by our company for this theatre, and they have lasted a long time. They look right and are quite comfortable. But successive groups of actors have found themselves sitting down in a pool of water which has gathered at the bottom of the curve! Anything painted has to be waterproof, and stay attached to the surface it is meant to be decorating. Nothing must be weakened or dissolved by water. Or for that matter sunshine!

The weather has one more trick in store for the set (and costume) designer. The wind forces can be terrific and are quite sufficient to blow over some pieces of furniture. High-backed chairs can be tipped over and small bits of furniture or props blown right off the stage. Any large piece which two men can lift easily may be quite unmanageable in a high wind without four times that number. We did, in fact, nearly have a hair-raising accident with the famous box containing Hermione. At one of the final rehearsals she had already entered the box when the wind started rocking it forwards and would have crashed it to the ground complete with actress if it had not been caught just in time by four technicians who rushed from the auditorium. After this incident we lashed the box back to the concrete with wire ropes. But it is easy to overlook these things if the weather is still and calm during rehearsal, or if rehearsal takes place elsewhere, as is the case with the majority of companies.

Two things of great importance in any production are lighting and sound. These are being dealt with from the technical angle in other chapters. From the director's point of view, however, lighting at the Minack can produce magical effects. The concrete picks up light superbly, and seems to absorb colour in a way which an ordinary set does not. The rough texture of the surface goes some way to explain this. But the director must keep his lighting in mind throughout rehearsals. The Minack does not possess an infinitely flexible lighting set-up, and if the director does not consult closely with the lighting designer during production he is likely to find himself unable to get the effects he wants. If he has some knowledge of the job himself this can be a great help in any theatre. On the Minack it can not only make the lighting designer's job a great deal easier, but make all the difference between demanding the improbable but possible, and the impossible!

Music and sound can contribute a great deal at the Minack. Quite apart from its usual uses, music is often technically necessary to 'cover' scene changes or time-consuming entrances. As you will have realised the theatre is very suitable for episodic plays with many changes of location which can be left largely to the audience's imagination, which is not always possible indoors. It is admirably suited to Elizabethan and Jacobean plays written in many scenes, and to more modern plays written on similar models. Music can do more to establish an atmosphere at the start of a scene and help the transition from place to place than the use of changing scenery or furniture. It has an immediate and powerful impact which somehow seems greater than its effect indoors. This is perhaps just because the actual setting is in a way 'neutral', and the audience picks up its cues from other things. At matinées especially, when there is (of course) no help from lighting, music is essential. It has a quite different sound in the open air, where there is no echo or resonance from the walls of the theatre or the set. Possibly because of this it is sometimes feasible to use music in a way which would be distracting in the indoor theatre. Some sounds often have a slightly artificial quality indoors. A trumpet call on the Minack has a 'reality' which it is difficult to achieve in a conventional theatre. A sound such as a gong or cymbal crash which sometimes sounds overdone indoors fits into the 'larger than life' quality of the theatre in a very special way. It is once again this ambiguity between the naturalistic and the 'oversize' which the director can exploit.

At last there comes the day when the company first moves on to the Minack stage to commence rehearsal. In the case of many companies the production is already rehearsed and more or less complete. This means that many of the problems I am going to write about in the next few pages will have been solved away from the theatre. This presents great difficulties, and I can only be glad that I have been so fortunate in this respect. All the productions I have done at the theatre have been worked out to a large extent on the stage itself. Even when we rehearse elsewhere, because another company is using the stage, we always know that in a day or so we can look at what we have done in its eventual setting. It would be well nigh impossible to mount the play in the time available—just ten days from start to finish—if this were not the case. Very intensive rehearsal, working many hours a day on the play, enables the director to work faster than is the case with most amateur productions, where a few days elapse between rehearsals and the cast have to carry on everyday affairs at the same time. It does, however, also bring its difficulties.

The first task which is done actually on a stage in the production of a play is blocking, that is working out the detailed moves which will be used. A great deal may have been done before, such as reading through the play as a company, discussing it and so on. This will, of course, vary from director to director. But eventually the time comes when cast, director and stage (in this case the actual stage rather than a rehearsal room) are brought together. Directors differ in the amount they work out in advance, and in the amount of detail they put in the first time they block a scene. I like to have at least the entrances and exits roughly plotted and to have decided the areas of the stage I shall use for the various scenes. Apart from this I have a set of mental pictures of how the stage will look at various times and some general ideas about various passages; this part I shall feel calls for tight, close grouping, this for open, well spread out grouping. But I do not like to plan the actual moves in advance, nor do I have a pre-arranged plan of how I shall get from one mental picture to another. And my mental pictures will usually only cover key moments. Generally I like actors to use the moves they feel comfortable with, and depend a great deal on them to determine for themselves the blocking we shall use. On the Minack this system has one enormous advantage. It allows us to be stimulated by the actual stage setting, and the feel and shape of the stage.

Perhaps because of this way of working, I always feel the problems and challenge of this stage particularly keenly in those first moments. As we walk down the steps leading to the auditorium and then to the stage I always feel a nervousness, an excitement mixed with apprehension. I mention this only because I am writing a personal account of directing at the Minack. I have no knowledge of whether other dirctors feel this. Certainly I get a similar feeling as I start rehearsal on any play anywhere, but it always feels sharper and more acute there. On this first morning I always enjoy watching the reactions of people who have never seen the theatre before and this may well add to the feeling of excitement. Sooner or later however the ice must be broken and we must start to rehearse, to block out the play.

The shape of the Minack stage and the position of its entrances and exits are somewhat extraordinary. As can be seen from the plans (back cover) the stage is very wide. At the left-hand side it is very shallow, whereas at the right it has become quite deep. Quite apart from the shape, a sort of egg with one side flattened, it has a number of obvious features. On the right-hand side is a slightly raised 'circle' of grass as opposed to the large tiles which floor the rest of the stage. This circle is a clearly defined area and can often be used as such. In the left centre is a slightly raised concrete platform, with two steps leading up to it, running back beyond the back line of the main stage and with two stairways leading up to it from below at the back. Behind the stage is the sea, and from the auditorium the stage looks as though it drops straight into the sea below. An actor jumping off the balustrade towards the sea appears to vanish down a steep cliff! The effect of this 'backdrop' is overwhelming at first sight, especially on a sunny day or fine evening. Contrary to appearances, there is a path backstage (or below-stage perhaps would be better). To the right of the dais is a vast stone 'table', affectionately known as the Fish-slab. Still further right at the back of the stage the low row of pillars which forms the back of the acting area ends with a pair of higher pillars and then there is a gap. Up into this gap runs a staircase from below-stage. On the extreme stage right, leading out of the circle are rocky steps leading right offstage, in fact to the dressing-room terrace. On the extreme left, the shallow end, the stage runs out on to a grassy terrace, unfortunately in view from only part of the auditorium, down a small step on to another smaller terrace and thus down steps at the extreme left (now out of sight to most of the audience) to the below-stage area. These last steps also run upwards, more or less out of sight up to the top of the auditorium. Just in front of the point where the stage proper gives on to this terrace is another flight of steps running up to the same position. There are thus seven standard entrances or exits, as marked on the stage plan.

In addition to these it is also possible to come down through the auditorium, arriving on the stage over the prompt box. Incidentally this prompt box is small and cramped, impossible to get in and out of during performances without being seen. As a result we have always dispensed with the services of a prompter, no highly literate, dramatically inclined gnome being available! There are a number of other features. Up on the rocks stage right but forward of the front edge of the stage is a niche which can be used for statues, gods and the like, and also a higher platform with similar possibilities. On the stage left a large platform beyond the terraces left of the stage proper can also be used, although audibility is a problem from here.

From this description and with the aid of the plans it will be clear that the theatre offers a wide range of possible entrances and exits, together with 'odd places' for special effects or purposes. On the stage itself are a number of other useful 'hazards'! There is a large rock well forward and far right which is a handy seat, and at either side of the steps leading up to the dais are two low blocks, or seats—always affectionately known as the Toad-stools for reasons which defeat me! There is also a sort of 'altar', stage right between the exit to the dressing-room and that to the depths below-stage, consisting of two tall pillars with a high piece in between them. Originally made as Tristan's

47

window in an early production it has a multitude of uses and can be approached from behind over the rocks giving another, if somewhat dangerous, entrance.

The theatre from this description would seem to be almost infinitely flexible, but alas there are a number of 'rules of the game' which come into play! It is not possible to get from stage left to right behind the stage area without coming into view. The alternative is to go from stage left round the back of the auditorium, which is a long way above the stage, down the backstage path to the dressing-room terrace and thus to the stage right entrance. This takes time and is exciting not to say dangerous in the dark! As a result a fairly lengthy time must elapse between a character disappearing on one side and reappearing on the other. Similar problems arise in getting from more or less any exit to a different entrance, and this must be allowed for when blocking. It is especially easy to give an actor an impossible task if for some reason scenes are blocked out of running order. Similarly, if a character goes off for instance stage right (up the steps) and in the next scene re-enters there, which is often called for, an unexpected difficulty can arise. The next scene may take place on the extreme stage left, leaving him a 40–50 ft walk before he enters the area being used!

To add to the delights of this particular game, parts of the stage are less visible than others from some parts of the auditorium. The extreme stage left is not in good view from the right-hand side of the audience because of the rake of the 'seats' which on that side are in fact grass rows. On the other hand some places are in all too good view! For example, actors entering from the centre steps can be seen from half-way up the steps. They cannot therefore wait just at the top of the steps ready for an immediate entrance but must 'time' their entrances from below. This sort of thing provides a problem which is peculiar to the Minack! Audibility is not very good from backstage, and with a wind blowing it may be impossible to hear an entrance cue, or more correctly the cue to come on from the sides of the stage or start up the steps. It then becomes necessary to be cued by another actor, by some visual sign, or by means of the backstage telephone system. A recent particularly tricky example occurred in our 1967 production of *A Man for All Seasons*. Two actors had to enter centre, arrive on stage on cue (which in this case was a particular spot in the music covering the scene change), and carry on a passage of dialogue with a good deal of action which had to end at exactly the right place for a trumpet cue. As the background music went on continually here, we had the trumpet call built into the tape, over the background music as it were. Once the whole sequence was started therefore it had to run exactly to time . . . 37 seconds I think it was! The scene change music was started, at a certain point the actors were cued, came up the steps and carried on the scene. If all went well, and I can happily record that it did, the trumpet call came in the right place. Had anything gone wrong . . . !

Despite these problems of access, visibility and audibility, which can be frustrating and require ingenuity to solve, the stage is very stimulating to work on. Actors can appear from many places and exit likewise. The stage can be split up into many areas, although it naturally falls into three main sections. One is the circle, the second the area left of it in front of the table, and the third the dais area, often called the throne area, which is ideal for formal indoor settings. The area left of this is very constricted, and visibility is not too good but for some purposes it is almost ideal. We used it for instance as the outhouse of the farm where King Lear shelters during the storm. It suggested, by its shape, a small crowded room, just off the storm-swept heath for which we had used the whole of the rest of the stage. Bringing actors through the audience can have a very strong effect as any director knows. The total absence of anything like a proscenium arch, and the position of the auditorium entirely above the stage and connected with it, heightens this effect. It is thus possible to draw the audience into the action to a great extent if desired. I tried to do this in the trial scene of *The Winter's Tale* by setting it in rather an unusual way.

49

The judge's chair, occupied by Leontes, was placed on the prompt box with his back to the audience. Hermione (in the dock) stood on the centre dais, between the pillars and bounded by the front step. On the concrete ledge which forms the footrest for the very bottom row of the audience I placed a few actors, spread round the arc of the auditorium. They attempted to draw the spectators around them into the action. An effect of sitting in the company of 'actor-members of the public' watching the trial of Hermione was thus created.

As soon as you start blocking on this stage you realise that as a result of its shape and that of the auditorium it is anything but conventional and stage 'pictures' can be built in all sorts of unorthodox ways. It is really like working in the 'semi-round'. The Minack is not a happy place for actors who cannot bear to turn their backs on any of their audience! One of the greatest delights for the director is the way in which scenes can be made to change shape by simply turning actors round but not necessarily moving them. A character entering centre (say) and all the others turning to face him as he attracts their attention can completely change the shape of the 'block', if for instance their interest was previously focused on an actor well stage right and upstage in the circle. The whole conception of up and downstage, of stage left and stage right becomes rather meaningless because of the curved stage front and the greater depth at stage right. Whereas an actor standing stage left must face more or less across the stage to address the audience, the actor stage right and well towards the sea has a fairly wide choice of angle. If he is standing in front of the 'altar' at the back of the circle he will feel that moving 'downstage' is moving on a diagonal line towards the middle of the auditorium, which strictly is partly downstage and partly stage left!

This is not, however, just a matter of juggling with terms. An actor learning a part has to learn more than words; very early on in rehearsal he has to learn moves. Some actors find it very hard to learn the one without the other. Now on a conventional stage a few actors 'place' themselves in relation to the setting, and learn their moves as 'go stage left' for instance. On the Minack where stage left always seems to be in a different place this is not very useful! Most actors, however, remember where they should be on the stage in relation to other actors, and this is fine, providing nothing goes wrong with one of the key figures in the 'block'. In practice on the Minack things go wrong very easily, much more easily than on ordinary stages. This is probably because its size both makes positioning difficult and produces a false sense of the size of the margin of error. Actors in this theatre actually have to be very sensitive to their position relative both to the set and the other actors, and in addition have to keep in mind that the curve of the auditorium will affect the angle at which they stand. Although the stage is very broad, it is not all that deep. Consequently it is fatally easy for a group to 'flatten out', and get in a straight line like a chorus line up, a dreadful sight! Unfortunately the whole audience is above stage level and as a result is very aware of the shape of the stage floor. As a director in this theatre you have to be acutely aware of this and realise that the shapes the audience sees on the floor are more important than they are in theatres where many of the audience are below stage level. The very breadth of the stage increases the tendency to get straight lines where they are not wanted, and both actors and director have to be constantly on their guard.

The stage has very little change of level, the dais, the circle and occasionally the Fish-slab, a Toad-stool or exceptionally a pillar being all that is available. Mercifully, the very angle of the auditorium which places such emphasis on the shape of the block means that change of level is less important, and a stronger effect can be achieved by having some actors sitting while others stand, using the various natural 'stools' as well as stage furniture and also sometimes using the stage floor itself. The actor is entirely visible even when lying down on the stage and this can often be exploited.

In any theatre the director will use his grouping to make dramatic points, but somehow on the Minack the shape of the group has extra power. Partly this is a matter of visibility but partly it is because the stage is so simple and uncluttered that the shapes show up clearly against it. Everything has a hard clean line, even the floor tiles. The eye is drawn irresistibly to consider the geometry of the scene before it.

One of the great difficulties in blocking a play there is that at first the theatre seems too flexible. There seems an almost infinite choice of areas, entrances and shapes. Opinion clearly will differ on this point, but I have always believed that this stage cries out for the use of the 'localising' technique. It is possible to use different parts of the stage to represent different places, and it is then possible to give the entrances and exits specific purposes. This exit leads out of the king's palace, that one to the river. Obviously in most plays of an episodic type one area on the stage will have to represent over the course of the play more than one area, but at least in this way some consistency of location is achieved. I have never been sure to what extent this is consciously worked out by an audience, but I am sure that they are affected by it. There is something disturbing in a production which uses one part of the stage for a particular place one minute, and another part for the same place at another time. Even if this is avoided and the whole stage used for all the scenes I believe this is confusing for an audience. The stage is so large that the eye cannot take it all in. Sometimes the audience will localise the stage for themselves if the director does not. And there is no guarantee that they will do it in a way of which he would approve! At night particularly, when the lights give a boundary to the areas the director has chosen, the effect can be very strong and the contrast between, say, a large open space and an indoor scene can be well suggested simply by using a very specific space for the latter and a large less well defined area for the former.

If this technique is used then immediately some order and discipline is introduced into the apparently over-abundant range of choices. In fact it can happen that to preserve the convention a particular entrance becomes over used, or a particular

Billy Rawlings, a master-hand with granite

The Priory Players' 1964 production of *Ondine* by Jean Giraudoux

West Cornwall Theatre Group's *Mary Stuart* by Schiller 1961

area appears too often! If the entire scheme is not to be scrapped and rethought, ingenuity may well be called for. Usually, of course, these areas are worked out in advance. When we did *A Man for All Seasons* I took this idea to its logical extreme and decided to delineate on the stage floor the edges of the various areas. I thought of a number of ways of doing this and rejected them all. Finally I hit on the idea of having three blockboard solid boxes, the size of the concrete blocks which mark the back of the stage. These were arranged on the stage in such a way that by moving one (or occasionally two) the acting area could be completely changed. In this play it happened to be easy to get them moved around (by the Common Man) and also fitted in with the nature of the character moving them. This indeed was what originally gave me the idea. I would be chary of doing it if 'scene-shifters' have to move the blocks, but the idea of actually marking out the areas seemed to work quite well.

Although, as I have tried to suggest, blocking the play is an important matter calling for a great deal of thought it is only after the play is blocked that rehearsal really starts! The first way in which rehearsal on the Minack differs from rehearsal in a room is remarkably obvious. Spending eight hours a day or more working on a play outside in the sun and rain is physically a different experience from doing the same thing indoors! We have found that from time to time it is necessary to work on certain scenes indoors in order to capture a particular atmosphere, later to be transferred if possible to the stage. It is far harder to achieve a high degree of concentration outdoors, and concentration is perhaps the most important thing both in rehearsal and performance.

In any production, on any stage, the director will aim at getting a tension which holds the audience gripped. This applies to comedy and tragedy alike. I am not talking of tension in quite the ordinary sense. What I am concerned with here is that quality in a play or a scene which compels the audience to watch it. This mysterious atmosphere is largely built up by concentration, every character on the stage acting all the time. Naturally one does not want the actor constantly moving about or changing facial expression in such a way that attention is drawn to him, perhaps at the expense of the character who should really be the focus of the audience's attention at that moment.

But, of course, every good actor knows the dangers of 'upstaging' a fellow actor. What seems to be less well understood even by highly competent amateur actors is the way in which tension is maintained, and the distressing ease with which a good scene can degenerate into a slack one. Given the chance the eye will scan the entire area before it from time to time, and will move about the centre of attention almost continually, resting more often on the object which is the focus of attention. It is most unusual for a member of an audience to stare fixedly at one point or one actor. Thus it follows that even if for most of the time a member of an audience is watching the actor (or group of actors) at that moment 'holding the stage', at the same time brief glances are taken at other parts of the stage. The audience may not really be conscious of making these eye movements, and some of the things observed may be out of the corner of the eye, just as many objects are seen in this way when driving a car. Nevertheless these peripheral objects are seen. Now, if they are behaving in the way expected then the eye will pass over them and the mind will not bother really to think about what was seen. The concentration of our member of the audience will remain fixed on whatever it is the players are attempting to present. But if the eye picks up behaviour which is somehow 'different', which does not fit in with the scene as a whole, then the attention is distracted and the tension of the scene is broken. I have gone into some detail on this point because it is one of the greatest challenges the director and his actors face on the Minack stage. Because of its size the eye can roam a long way from the centre of the scene without leaving the stage and going 'out of bounds' as it were. This can best be grasped by thinking how much simpler it is to take in the picture on a television set than on a conventional indoor stage. Being much larger than most indoor stages used by amateurs the problem at the Minack is even more acute. And this is quite apart from the fact that if the eye strays off the stage the surrounding scenery is a superb combination of sea and sky, cliffs and bays! It is rather important therefore on this stage to 'bound' scenes and ensure by the way the play is blocked and set on the stage that there is something to stop the travelling eye before it leaves the area of attention. Actors must be discouraged from turning away from a group if they are themselves on the outside edge of it, unless the action really contributes something. This is because it leaves an opening and in following the actor's gaze the eye can be drawn out of the group and away across the stage or off it.

This concentration all sounds very straightforward and easy to achieve. And sitting here in my study, 600 miles from the Minack on a sunny winter's day, it does indeed seem very simple! Actors, however, are human beings. Rehearsing day after day for hours on end in a theatre which can be freezing cold, swept with wind and rain one minute and roasting in a temperature of 80 degrees the next, is a physical strain. The sort of concentration and attention to detail which is needed to maintain tension (and the audience's attention) is tiring at the best of times. Inevitably there are moments when the actor is tempted to relax, float along on the wave of the scene. And this can happen in performance as well as in rehearsal. And it is fatal to that elusive quality which marks a really good scene, act or play. Nor is it true that this quality of concentration can be acquired suddenly at the end of a series of rehearsals in which the actors have been coasting along, reserving themselves for the final effort. It has to be built into the production, day by day and each time the scene is rehearsed. It is one of the director's most arduous and important tasks to give his production this tightness and concentrated finish. And on the Minack his task is greater than usual.

Of course this theatre is no different from others in that all the other processes of rehearsal have to be gone through. Each scene is worked over, details are added, business is put in, the actors discuss it section by section, and sometimes line by line. And all the time the director must try to keep his eye on that most elusive of all a play's features: its shape. When the finished play is seen at last by the audience they will have no difficulty in appreciating the shape if it is there. And they will sense if it is not, even if they cannot put their dissatisfaction into those words. For the director who necessarily works on the play piecemeal, sometimes with the scenes out of their running order, it is very easy to lose sight of the overall pattern he is attempting to create. It is easy to become obsessed with detail, to lose the wood in the trees. This is where the constraints of time will be felt particularly keenly. There is never quite enough time to rehearse a play, no matter how long the rehearsal period! But given the time pressure at the Minack I know that I shall only get one bite at the cherry, that I must get the shape set more or less right in the early rehearsals. By the time I see the play complete at the first run-through it will be difficult to change its entire pattern, although many smaller changes can and will be made. I always try to have the first run-through as early as possible, in some ways earlier than is ideal, so that I can have a look at the play as a whole and give myself the longest possible time to make corrections.

The first run-through is an important occasion. We shall probably have the sound effects and music for the first time. The material is all recorded in advance and the sound technician who will work the show has discussed the cues with me beforehand. There are, however, always many alterations of detail which have to be made, and the first run-through is often the occasion I use to find out some of the snags. We shall have a full sound rehearsal to set the final sound levels and make sure everything is right a little later in rehearsals. This first 'run' is also the first opportunity the lighting designer will have to see the play in its entirety, straight through. Before this we have discussed the lighting in general terms and he will probably have attended some rehearsals. But this is his first chance to start plotting the lighting in detail, to decide where he will hang his lamps and so on. The Minack is not the easiest of places to light so this is an important rehearsal for him.

For me the first run-through is one of the most exciting of all the rehearsals. The play half takes life for the first time. The actors go through uninterrupted, barring disasters, without scripts, scene following scene as it will eventually do in performance. It is at this moment that the play begins to acquire that autonomy, a sort of self-generated life which will take over at the end of rehearsals. All really good performances have a certain momentum. There is an inevitability, once the play has started, that it will move on, carried by its own inner power and tension until finally the actors leave the stage for the last time. At this first run-through I am both trying to assess this momentum to see if the overall shape and pace of the play is right, and also to decide how the life that is there can be encouraged.

From now on the pace seems to quicken more and more. The short period available for the detailed rehearsals flies by. The second run-through. More adjustments of detail. Technical rehearsals for sound and lighting, the latter generally requiring a night out of bed for the technical crew, and for me. The first dress rehearsal, last minute changes, the second dress rehearsal. Final notes after the second dress rehearsal, my last chance to affect the play. But to be honest I know that once the play has reached dress rehearsal it is very difficult to do more than smooth out the flow. There is no longer any real chance to alter the shape, the pace, or even a performance. The die is really cast. Nevertheless there are always small points to adjust after dress rehearsals, and after the second one I give my notes with a sense of finality. For better for worse the play is completed as far as I am concerned. It is now up to the actors. The fate of the play as I have conceived it, as well as their own individual fate as performers is in their hands. All I can do is spend Monday trying not to worry about the first performance!

At the Minack I am a fortunate man in that after my task as

director ends I generally change into a technician for the dura-
tion of the run. I find that this creates a marvellous sense of
detachment! So I can honestly report that once the play starts
I am not a bag of nerves. But there is something very exciting
about going down to the theatre early on the Monday evening,
making the final technical checks and then watching the audience come in. I wish I could report that the first performance
always occurs on a perfect evening, with a clear sky and the sun
setting spectacularly behind the auditorium. Alas, it sometimes
rains, even heavily. Sometimes it is a wild night with the wind
howling and the sea high. Sometimes there is a mist which
actually creates a magic all its own as the lights are reflected
back by the drops of water and the stage acquires a distant,
almost magical quality. But let us suppose that tonight it is a
perfect evening and the audience coming down the path into the
theatre have spent a day on the sun-drenched beaches. The sea
is calm and the evening windstill. The opening music is heard, the
play unfolds. Watching from the lighting box I feel somehow a
different person. Although I only ceased directing the play the
previous evening it already seems a long time ago. There is a
very definite sense in which, for the director, the performance is
an incidental, the finish to a process but not the process itself. I
do enjoy watching plays I have directed, at least sometimes, but
the involvement is nothing like as great as might be expected.
On the first night of course there is a great thrill of expectation,
the wish to see whether it will after all turn out the way one
hoped, or whether despite everyone's efforts it is just not going
to work out right. Curiously enough this may be quite independent of whether the play has a great success. It is quite possible
for a play to enjoy considerable success but not look as its
director wanted it. And the reverse is also true. Sometimes one
achieves exactly what one wanted and nobody likes it! Happily
both can occur together and the play not only turns out as one
wanted it, but people like it too. And yet . . . it never *quite* turns
out as one hoped. There is always a bit here, a section there,
which is wrong. Too slow, too quick, not intense enough, over

pitched, badly blocked, flowing badly, unclear, dull, or just plain wrong and no-one quite knows why!

Thus it is that in the evening six days later, when the actors have all made their way up the cliff path and I stand looking at the empty theatre, one of the thoughts in my mind is always 'Now, if . . .'! No director is ever quite satisfied and it is this, combined with the breath-taking beauty of the theatre and the fact that there are hundreds of good plays I have hardly read, let alone directed, that makes me sure at that very moment that I shall come back. A last look around as I remember guiltily that some of the company are, no doubt, waiting for a lift back from the theatre to our temporary home in St Just. A little sadly I leave the theatre, plodding up the cliff path to the car. We drive out of the car park, along the bumpy track to the road. Another Minack season is over. I shall return to Edinburgh, probably to direct at least one play and to work on others during the year, but for me nothing can quite equal the Minack. It is the most challenging, most exciting, most frustrating and most loved theatre I have ever worked in. It has become an integral part of my life.

CHAPTER 3

Acting at Minack—
A Personal Impression   TIM CRIBB

> *Actors*
> *You who perform plays in great houses*
> *Under false suns and before silent faces*
> *Look sometimes at*
> *The theatre whose stage is the street.*

Brecht never came to a matinée at Minack. He would have found the point of his exhortation blunted if he had, for there the street is, sitting in rather restless rows under a sometimes all-too-real sun, complete with its dogs, children, ice-creams, and miscellaneous accidents of life. It's hard to project the illusions of the imagination on to an audience so blatantly living in the everyday world. Why should it suspend its continuity for the make-believe of a play? In the dark, in a great house dedicated to make-believe, magically isolated in stage light, an actor can mould the audience like a plastic mass and the audience expectantly yields. But in common daylight he becomes a common man. It is plain for all to see that he inhabits the same world under the same sky and presumably lives by the same twenty-four hour clock as everyone else. An actor leaves his dressing-room and instead of a king stepping on to the stage it is a strayed member of the audience, nodding and speaking to them with all the conflicting impulses of sociability and slight embarrassment.

He is likely to be most painfully conscious of this in plays

62

which deliberately incorporate a game of touch and run with the bounds of fiction. Consider these lines from *The Winter's Tale*:

> Many a man there is (*even at this present,*
> *Now, while I speak this*) *holds his wife by the arm,*
> *That little thinks she has been sluiced in's absence,*
> *And his pond fished by his next neighbour* (*by*
> *Sir Smile, his neighbour*).

As the actor raises his arm preparatory to pointing at some anonymous patch of darkness in the stalls he is liable to find his gesture arrested by the actual sight of Sir Smile with a peeling nose and radiating the security of unconscious innocence, or, worse, the reverse. To point at actual people and accuse them in public of adultery is bad manners, especially if true. What is he to do? With good luck and good sense and good direction he may reach the conclusion that the gesture was a mere actor's reflex anyway, perhaps originating in the cheap thrill of breaking taboos in the dark. So he leaves it out. And the audience remain audience. And the play makes its own point, not the actor's. All of which comes down to saying that acting at Minack is a disciplining experience.

At the most elementary level common to all theatres the Minack imposes certain crude mechanical laws which the actor must obey if he is to be seen and heard. With the audience banked so steeply above the stage, it is forbidden to adopt the hunched posture and pregnant scrutinizing of the hands and figures which hallmarks some Method-style performers: all most of the audience can see is the ineloquent top of your head. Similarly, a trio of actors in an animated conversational huddle, occasionally shooting out an arm or stepping back on one leg, resembles nothing so much as one of those little wood platters of hens which peck up and down as you gyrate the weight beneath them. Conversations have to be carried on not at the shoulder height of normal life but with what feels like a quite artificial elevation of the chin and Young Lochinvar illumination of the brow. This rule is equivalent to the indoor theatre one which says that when turning away from the audience to speak to a person upstage you can in fact aim your speech 45 degrees downstage of his ear and still look quite natural, whilst of course being much more effortlessly heard. How easy to decree! How hard for the occasional amateur to learn to obey!

Holding one's head up naturally increases one's chances of being heard, but on the Minack the chances still remain low. To begin with, the combination of the exceptional width of span of the seating with the exceptional length and irregularity of depth of the stage means that it's very difficult to cover the whole of the auditorium with your voice from all positions at all times. This difficulty is aggravated by a propensity of romantically inclined members of the audience to eschew seats in favour of perches on crags and private retirements in nooks and clefts of rock, and, although seemingly contented enough in such retreats, who is to know whether they may not feel cheated of their money if, on tiring of murmuring sweet nothings to themselves, they turn to hear something of the play, and can't? Then there's the sea; and the weather; and the two of them in hostile alliance—so that what with geomorphology, lovers, and atmospherics, an actor may be excused for feeling like crying 'Help!' waving a forlorn hand, and going under. Moreover, as the wife says in domestic comedies, shouting won't do you any good at all; for wind and sea, like wives, are adversaries who tire not, and a man pits himself against them in vain. With a little cunning one can sometimes make these recalcitrant features of nature work for instead of against one. There is a particular crag on the right of the auditorium, for instance, off which one can bounce one's voice, and since Miss Cade covered most of the stage in delicately tinted concrete hexagons it has become a better sounding board, while intuitive course-track-drift estimates can be made to allow for the wind. But, if you don't want to tear a passion and your throat to tatters, if you want to preserve any natural quality, colour and flexibility in your speech, there is no substitute for correct voice production. Even then, weather conditions may be such that while you bellow intimacies

and half-stun your fellow actors with throwaways and under-
cuts, remoter members of the audience get the impression that
'These our actors, As I foretold you . . . Are melted into air,
into thin air.'

It is difficult under any Minack conditions to speak the words
trippingly with that light, dry, timbre which carries quietly to
the farthest wall of indoor theatres, and this inevitably conditions the phrasing, rhythm and tempo of one's acting. Prose,
particularly modern prose, seems harder to deliver than verse.
In verse plays the more obvious rhythmic shaping of the
speeches and scenes preserves and carries the overall meaning,
while the tendency of verse lines to lift towards the end gives
them better carrying power than the naturalistically falling
sentence rhythms of modern dialogue. Consequently, the responsibility for the delineating of the play's rhythm is thrown
more squarely on the director's shoulders than perhaps is the
case with indoor theatres. If this surmise is correct then we have
another instance of the clarifying and impersonal rigour of
Minack's disciplines.

Another of its disciplines is the impossibility of having a complicated set with all the bric-á-brac of bourgeois life. Now it is a
great comfort to the poor shrinking human personality to find
itself supported and amplified, as it were, by an extension of
itself. Since the rise of the novel (or is it of the middle classes?)
we have been trained to read furniture, and to interpret a family's
history from the appearance of its living-room. No such signi-
ficant excrescence is possible at Minack. All there is of this kind
is costume—and acting. The difference of indoor and outdoor
scenes, the variations of the year and the weather, the forest of
Arden and a wood outside Athens, midnight and dawn, publicity and privacy—all must principally be created by the varying
language of the actor's body and by the differing gestures of his
voice.

Apart from the set, it is also a great comfort to have a few
props to clutch at in moments of distress, or to fill in patches
where there seems nothing particular to do. Every performance

is stretched over the abyss of the 'dry', that panic black-out when one suddenly realises one has no idea of what's coming next. There is always the possibility that Blondin will fall into Niagara. Well, this being the nature of acting, it's nice to know that one can cover up by lighting a cigarette, pouring a drink, or examining some *objet*, and such knowledge both diminishes the chances of drying, and, should it occur, the covering action in the process of restoring confidence often restores memory, or at least gives a fellow actor the chance to prompt.

I have myself had occasion, an occasion that only Minack could have created, to be grateful for such scanty props as it allows. The scene was one of the rebel councils of war in *Henry IV*. In it the leading rebs have a vigorous disagreement about tactics and then, according to the text, 'The trumpet sounds to parley' and enter Sir Walter Blunt (to parley). He didn't. . . . Fortunately we had a map, so, hastily improvising some rather blank verse,

> *Let us consult the map !* (said I)
> *And make our dispositions for the day . . .*

which we did, save for the Scots reb, who decided it would be more in character to stump off in dudgeon and leave the other three of us to improvise by ourselves (we spoke to him about that afterwards). Having muttered over the map a little I felt that we ought to act as if some sort of decision had been reached, thus promoting the illusion of still acting Shakespeare, and accordingly rolled the map up rather rudely (but in character) and marched over to a parapet to survey the horizon (which was sheer cowardice). Worcester, however, malevolent in all aspects (that is both in and out of character), feigned to be struck by sudden thought, marched after me to the parapet, spun me round, and holding me at arm's length the way actors in Shakespeare do to indicate sincerity, asked, very loudly, 'Whence comes the king?' I hadn't the faintest idea. Not only did the panic darkness descend but the whole illusion collapsed, because what I in fact uttered in my startlement was an all-too-natural

sounding 'er' followed by blank silence. Fortunately the trumpet sounded to parley again, and this time Sir Walter appeared,
himself rather startled by the fervour of his welcome. What had
happened was that in making his entrance down through the
audience he had met some parents at the top who were taking
their child home. The resisting child, its imagination possibly
heated by too much Malory, had fled to Sir Walter for help,
clutched him round the knees, and lengthened his journey to the
rebel camp by the vital thirty seconds. Hazards of this kind are
yet another feature of Minack life from which most actors are
safely insulated.

From one point of view, then, acting at Minack is particularly
trying and difficult, but from another it is a matter for rejoicing,
since this is what the game is all about. After all, how infinitely
boring the business with the cigarettes, the telephone, the tea-
cups! How tiresome, how trivial, how 'camp' the knowing
adjustment of speech to the elegant drawing on of a pair of
gloves in Wilde or the taking of snuff in Goldsmith! (And also,
it must be admitted, *how* elegant, *how* suave, *how* delightful!)
What's the point of watching Blondin if there's no chance of his
falling into Niagara? One of the peculiar energies of the theatre
(as distinct from the cinema) is that it involves real people living
from moment to moment in a state of risk, risk that the pretence
will collapse, the illusion be exposed as a fraud, the whole gamble
fail, and the game seem a set of ridiculously arbitrary conventions. This is perhaps why, at a certain level of acting, the more
you permit yourself to become absorbed in the part and to enter
the acting dream, the greater the risk of the conscious prompting
mind being laid completely to sleep so that it is not there to take
over should some minor crisis occur; the dreamer is suddenly
awake, bewildered, or, in stage terms, the actor is thrown. Since
props and sets are in some ways a protection against this, and
since theatre thrives on danger, to my mind there is a Greek or
Elizabethan simplicity about Minack's stage conditions which
forces one back on essentials.

This lack of equipment is, then, a negative virtue of Minack, a virtue which has its effect on movement too. To begin with the disadvantages, there are the natural hazards of the rocks, particularly for women in long dresses. To make a running entrance down the steps stage right requires considerable deftness of footing. I remember one of our prettier actresses inflicted lamentable temporary ugliness on her nose when she fell on it in trying to do just this, and Lear once missed a step and all but dropped Cordelia, while as for the hazards of the various rough-hewn ascents and goat tracks back stage, they are beyond description.

I have mentioned the peculiar relationship between actor and audience at a Minack matinée, and I shall return to this presently. There is also a peculiar relationship between the actor's body and the Minack itself, or rather, between his body and the extensive area of the English Channel bounded by the Lizard on the one hand and by the Atlantic on the other. It is unusual to have to act against the Atlantic. It is indeed intimidating. Once on stage, an actor may well be demoralised by a feeling of total exposure and insignificance, particularly if all he has to do is cross it from one end to the other. Just as the absence of props and naturalistic sets deprives him of psychological support, so the extraordinary length of the stage, backed by the mere emptiness of sky, deprives him of literal physical support. So much of our bearing and what used to be called deportment is conditioned by the tables we rest our elbows on, the armchairs we relax in, the kitchen and household equipment we stoop over and push around that it requires a considerable adjustment of the carriage to look like an animal used simply to walking and standing. One is reminded of W. B. Yeats's comparison of a Renaissance portrait with Sargent's portrait of President Wilson:

> Whatever thought broods in the dark eyes of that Venetian gentleman, has drawn its life from his whole body; it feeds upon it as the flame feeds upon the candle—and should that thought be changed, his pose would change, his very cloak would rustle for his whole body thinks. President Wilson lives only in the eyes, which are steady and intent; the flesh

above the mouth is dead, and the hands are dead, and the clothes suggest no movement of his body, nor any movement but that of the valet, who has brushed and folded in mechanical routine. There, all was an energy flowing outward from the nature itself; here, all is the anxious study and slight deflection of external force. . . .

Every play and every period has its implicit code of gesture and physical style. Similarly, a theatre will dictate the style of acting appropriate to itself. At Minack the vastness of the space in which the actor's body moves means that the subtler facial gestures, minimal motion of a muscle to indicate a larger movement by its supression, the whole repertoire of expression based on the assumption that the actor is so closely watched that merest velleities will betray him, in short the cinematic style of acting—all this scrupulous craftsmanship goes for nothing. Gestures to be effective must be seen, and this means on the Minack that they must have both scale and time to make themselves felt. This presents considerable problems for an actor who has to portray, say, vacillation and uncertainty, for too much dithering in such a setting looks ridiculous. At a purely technical level, then, the Minack encourages a rather broader, simpler and clearer, perhaps more rhetorical style than an indoor actor is likely to be accustomed to. But there is more to it than just that.

There is the sheer competition from one of the more overwhelming pieces of scenery on the English coastline, whether by day, when it is perpetually transforming itself under the light, or by darkness, when the moon climbs over the Logan, and lighted ships pass up the Channel, and the sound of waves becomes compellingly insistent on the ear. It is the *presence* of this coastscape, its magisterial personality, which diminishes the scale and annihilates the personality of the actor. To fight against it is clearly impossible. Technique can vanquish wind and waves to the extent of making oneself audible, but to seem bigger than them, to dominate and possess the scene (the word takes an interesting twist in this extra-theatrical context), to loom and menace as one can in an indoor theatre is not within human power. The competition is deaf, unmodifiable, indifferent to the individual: Minack is not the stage for solo performances. And here again, to state the problem in these terms is to reveal its intrinsic answer.

To the degree that Minack does not lend itself to solos, it offers correspondingly rich returns on ensemble playing. It is precisely because the individual is so devalued by the emptiness around him that a premium is set upon playing together. An actor should therefore expend his resourcefulness and imagination on exactly defining the location of the scenes in time and place, and on exactly defining his relationship with the other characters. This means he will spend a good deal of time examining not just his own speeches but those of the other characters he has to deal with, for it is only by suggesting a dense reciprocity of relationship that the play will acquire its substance and weight. The more the audience feel that the characters are real to each other and that the situations they are in have urgency and familiarity to them, the more it will come to believe in the illusion of the play, which will consequently begin to live and grow until it usurps the reality of the outside world. This also means that one of the hardest things for an actor to do on the Minack is to start a play. It is very difficult to enter on such a setting and impose a play's reality cold, as it were, on a rather scattered audience. Indoors, an expectant hush descends with the lights and the curtain rises to reveal a complete world already in existence; but at Minack the natural world calmly persists, and even at night the lights don't begin to tell until some way through the first act. For the same reason, the illusion, once achieved, is precariously held. Such is the nature of the stage that it needs only one courtier to relax his vigilance and the whole reality of the scene leaks away, or, put the other way round, if one actor ceases to concentrate he makes a gap in the defences of art and nature rushes into the vacuum.

In other words, the great end to be sought after is that the characters should be as it were enclosed in the play, completely absorbed in a world of their own, prisoners of the story. When

A break in rehearsal—Penzance Playgoers' Theatre Club production of *The Lady's not for Burning*. Porthcurno Bay and the Logan Rock in the background

Shakespeare's *Measure for Measure* performed by Cambridge University Players in 1961

this illusion is achieved there is a great pathos at their oblivious-
ness of the world outside through their blind absorption with
their fates, and, at the height of the illusion, the play world does
command the scene: nothing comes amiss to it, all accidents are
incorporated into it, everything is necessary and nothing matters.
It seems to me that at these rare moments, what can be achieved
on Minack is almost qualitatively beyond what can be achieved
indoors, almost as if there were a law that the greater the resis-
tances to be overcome, the greater the reward. Perhaps a version
of the pathetic fallacy is activated, and the audience feel that not
only it, but the elements are watching, restoring life to the
Ancient Greek image of Night-with-a-thousand-eyes. As for the
actor, he must turn his back on the scene, and concentrate in-
tensely on his acting.

There is no recipe for concentration so one can only resort to
moral exhortation, like politicians do when they propound such
maxims as 'The price of democracy is eternal vigilance,' not of
course against an exterior enemy, but against one's own sloth.
If this opinion is accepted, then once again it seems to me
that the responsibility for judging the strategy of a given play
is clearly given to the director. It is he who has to decide on
the nature of the adjustment between the given play and the
Minack.

This was first brought home to me in our production of *Lear*.
We had the usual thunder and perhaps rather less than the usual
lightning, and the actors spent a lot of rehearsal time on miming
reactions to violent gusts of wind. During the storm scenes they
were beaten hither and thither across the stage and, as one critic
commented, looked quite small. Now, the alternative to a 'real'
storm is a mental storm, where the thunder and lightning are
deemed to be a magnifying symbol of Lear's mind. Yet on the
Minack, actors favouring such an interpretation would continue
to look quite small, and in such a case, *inappropriately* so: for no
one can kid you that the real sea and sky are only aspects of his
mind when they are actually present. But, although you can't
win if you pit yourself against the elements, you can exploit their

E   73

presence if you suggest that there is an element of attitudinising and acting in Lear's apostrophies, and this way they become, to the degree that he confuses the reality of the elements with the reality of his mind, a measure of his madness. In our production Lear in the storm did look small, as is unavoidable at Minack, but appropriately so. The world of the play was not preserved only, but created out of its relationship with its setting. In a very deep-lying and physical way, then, acting on the Minack if it is to be successful demands a right understanding of the relationship between actor, play, and setting, whether intuitive or deliberate and, since most productions are for only one week at a time and at yearly intervals, it is probably best if the adjustment is deliberate, at least on the producer's part.

Just as important and special to the Minack is the particular nature of the relation between actor and audience, indeed it is a product of the physical conditions. The relationship has two aspects. The auditorium descends to the stage in steps so that members of the audience can, if they choose to occupy the very last step, rest their feet on the same surface as the actors, or, from the other point of view, the actors can join the audience simply by sitting down on the edge of the stage. Everyone thus shares the same space, which has the character more of a part of nature than of a theatre. There is no marked physical division between spectator and actor and so a less distinct mental division than obtains indoors. This physical and psychological proximity must inevitably be of consequence for the acting. For instance, to deal with the most obvious first, make-up has to be both sufficiently natural-looking to be acceptable by the front row, and sufficiently emphatic to be observable by the top row, which means that line work is on the whole wasted, and a modelling technique has to be adopted.

A certain artificiality is part of the theatre, but children are, of course, the most intolerant critics of verisimilitude in certain matters, and their refusal to compromise with stage conventions can be embarrassing. It is a good maxim for any box office manager not to let younger brothers of company members sit in the front row. I base this advice on the experiences of an elder brother in our company who, freshly slain in one of the scenes of carnage at the end of *Henry IV*, all but sprang back to vengeful life on hearing in his ears a penetratingly familiar whisper, 'I can see you breathing'. The nearest parallel to this that I can remember is from an unruly school matinée at the Old Vic when Macbeth in the middle of 'Tomorrow and tomorrow and tomorrow' interjected a savage 'Shut up!' We did shut up, and this leads to the second aspect of the actor-audience relationship—at Minack they probably wouldn't.

I say this because, paradoxically, at the same time as the actors feel less distinctly separated from the audience than they would indoors, the audience feels more remote from the actors. Because the spectators are conscious of occupying the same world as the actors, they surrender less of themselves to the actors' usurpation of reality. Instead of abandoning themselves to the mass response or to worship or to passivity, they remain relatively self-possessed and critical. The steep banking up of the seats reinforces the audience's feeling of itself as circles of superior beings looking judicially down on the action below. I have already quoted Brecht in referring to this relationship. At first glance it might seem that such a theatre would suit his idea of the actor:

> *He's no sleep walker you may not address,*
> *Nor high priest at service.*
> *Interrupt as you will.*
> *Calmly he will reply.*
> *And when you have had your say*
> *Continue his performance.*

I do not in fact feel that such exchanges would go happily on the Minack. The point is that Brecht wants his actors to feel alienated, to feel detached and critical about the characters they are portraying; but at Minack it's the audience that feels alienated, so that Brecht's job is done for him. And it is by concentrating inwards, by absorbing themselves in the world of the play that the actors co-operate with the effect. Brecht argues that

Acting at Minack

By creating this distinction between yourselves and the world
You banish yourselves from the world

and in certain theatrical circumstances one can see that that
would be pernicious. But at Minack there is no such danger: the
tawdry or self-indulgent make-believe of some theatres and
actors is immediately exposed for what it is. In other words, because of the audience-relationship (as well as the setting) the
alienation effect will operate willy-nilly and if an actor fails to
co-operate with it he will be its victim. Yet again we come back
to the inherent disciplines of the Minack.

The detachment of the audience works to different effects with
different plays, of course, but the important thing is to understand and exploit it. Trials, for instance, though practically fool-
proof on any stage or screen, are particularly effective at Minack
since they can draw on the audience's idea of itself. The attitude
of the audience towards scenes of suffering and anguish is of a
Lucretian, contemplative kind—pity and pathos rather than
suffering itself. It's not that the audience's withers are unwrung,
but that it has as it were a more medieval attitude towards
tragedy: looks down from heaven weeping instead of up in awe
and terror. Part of this pathos comes from its impotence to
intervene, a feeling that rises in proportion to the audience's
feeling of alienation, which is in turn dependent on its feeling of
being excluded from the world of the play. The actor, then, must
concentrate on living in this world; his style should be centripetal
rather than centrifugal. Otherwise the audience will not take his
sufferings seriously and the detachment can turn to indifference.
In comedy, naturally, this does not obtain to the same extent,
but the alienation effect continues to modify the end product
nonetheless. Comedy of situation, particularly when expressed
physically, comes across very clearly because the audience is in a
position to see the situation diagrammatically exposed on the
stage below them. Comic rogues who seek to ingratiate themselves with the audience are readily accepted, but with an
amused, tolerant detachment which will prevent dramatically
undue concern when they get their comeuppance—provided the

'serious' characters are adequate vehicles of the play's overall intention. Insincerity, posturing, and indeed many personal inadequacies are coolly exposed.

If this description should sound too belittling, too diminishing to the actor, I can only say that the satisfaction gained from playing with (or deliberately against) the nature of the theatre is, if not identical with that of playing indoors, at least as keen. An instance that occurs to me from our own experience is when Lear discovers his servant Kent in the stocks and cannot believe his own daughter responsible, so that Kent has to repeat his assertion four times. It seemed to us in rehearsal that the scene was a cruel sort of comedy and in performance the audience-reaction confirmed this, for each of Kent's laconic repetitions brought a burst of laughter as the ludicrousness of the situation was brought home, while at each of Lear's denials we could feel the audience swing round from laughter to concern. The Minack point of this is that the audience was able to switch between the two attitudes with such agility because each was based on an understanding of the situation, a different understanding for each response, and the audience understood by virtue of its detachment, and that is what I mean by saying that the Minack audience is critical. The point for an actor is that playing the scene this way yielded as much pleasure as a more imposing interpretation would have done. There was a technical pleasure in perfecting the timing of each change of mood. There was a competitive pleasure in the clash of personality between character and character, actor and actor. There was a pleasure in hearing that the audience was really there and reacting in such full measure. There was a pleasure in flirting with laughter in an overall situation of gathering darkness. And there was the exhilarating pleasure of feeling that the play was alive, that the situations were charged and the emotional dynamics working, that the whole thing was moving inexorably forward and carrying us with it.

What one cannot do on the Minack is menace or threaten the audience—fellow characters yes, but not the spectators. In the last resort the tolerance and the detachment is a result of the audience's security in being above the actors and installed in the same world, and that cannot be shaken. The audience can be shaken literally, of course, for I remember an apprehensive husband exclaiming 'Steady on now' as the last battle of *Henry IV* swept past his nose, but that really only proves my point. At least I hope it does, for after all this I suppose someone will produce Pinter with spine-chilling success and I shall have to eat my words.

Indeed, all of this earnest speculation is perhaps rather fanciful. Perhaps the really important things for an actor at Minack are stamina, agility and a sangfroid that will enable him to preserve an attitude of elegant relaxation suggestive of summer in Illyria, or an impression of domestic intimacy suggestive of Desdemona's bedroom while water spreads osmotically through his tights or rain trickles down the neck of her nightgown. This is in fact quite a serious point. It is no good coming to Minack if you really are frail and flower-like, although it is quite all right to look frail and flower-like, should you wish to, on stage. The basic challenge of the Minack is a physical one. You have to be able to sustain not only your part but the exposure and the sheer taxing of energy involved in working such an arduous theatre. The stage is such that it will not permit you to coast through a scene. Backstage is such that you have an energetic climb in order to cross from left to right. Dressing-room accommodation is primitive; and anyway circumstances may dictate that your quick change has to be done behind a rock with only a mirror and one wind-swung light bulb. Yet possibly the best thing that Minack ever did to our company was to mount a real storm in the dress rehearsal in our first year. Partly through fear of failure in our first production in such novel conditions, partly through sheer excitement at acting in a storm we managed to ride it out. Subtlety went by the board, but the play survived, indeed it was born alive and kicking, out of that very challenge (it was *The Taming of the Shrew*).

The truth is that to put up with Minack's conditions is not

enough, you have to enjoy them, and why be in amateur theatre at all if not for enjoyment? Wind and rain and cold are not in fact as difficult to cope with as one might think. If the production has succeeded in creating a self-absorbed world out of the play, then one can enter it and, turning one's back on the elements, forget the cold; while the persistence of the audience against such odds is a great support too. Far more trying for both audience and actors is the broiling matinée when the sun beating on the concrete stage and concrete circles of seats makes the Minack into an inferno. This is probably because the audience finds it much harder to watch concentratedly in the intense light while the actors find it difficult to concentrate on their characters while squinting. However, that is the Minack, and while one man's meat is another man's poison, true, surely it is not too exotically perverse to find pleasure in meeting this kind of challenge.

I see I have waxed portentous again. Setting all psychologising and analysing aside, what more splendid setting for a busman's holiday could one imagine? After all, Cornwall is one of the main holiday attractions of the British Isles, and we enjoy the benefit of this with the added *piquant* of superiority to the holiday-makers pure and simple, weighed down with the responsibility of being on holiday and having to enjoy themselves, by virtue of our being in Cornwall for a purpose. Putting on plays in a holiday centre is but an elaborate stratagem to outflank the Puritan pleasure-censor in all of us by pretending that the whole enterprise is for other people's enjoyment rather than our own. This doublethink comes with the bonus of imparting a proprietary interest in the locality so that we feel more like residents than visitors, or at least like an amphibious species between the two. Perhaps the nearest analogy is to the nineteenth-century English in the South of France. We love the country and its people and preserve a due *hauteur* towards mere itinerant birds of passage, yet remain aware that it is not our country or our people; the Cornish remain inscrutably friendly and impenetrably hospitable, for which we like them. And what people! But our chief acquaintance is in pubs and this is not the place for that kind of reminiscence, so I will instead exclaim, And what country! However busy the week of the performance there is always time for a quick visit to one of the fishing villages, or a walk along the cliffs, or a further exploration of Penzance. However crowded the rehearsal schedule, there is time for a quick dip in the sea from Minack Rock or Porthcurno beach. Few theatres can be so fortunately placed for an actor's non-acting pleasures.

Besides the enjoyment we share with everyone else who comes to Cornwall, there are certain extras derived from being members of a company. One of the best means to friendship is a shared enterprise: it provides a simplifying medium for relationships both impersonal and intimate, like that of children at play, though with the benefit of adult consciousness of others. The objective to be achieved provides the standard by which one's fellows are analysed and evaluated and this removes the odium of personal animus, while people's proficiencies and deficiencies of talent and character can all be included as complementary parts of the whole, in our case the play. (Clearly this applies to the entire company, so I am no longer thinking exclusively as an actor.) Yet at the same time as our relationships are what I believe the sociologists call functionally specific, they are unusually close—literally: if the play of the year has a large cast, then you can't get out of bed at the side in the morning, only at the foot. For all the spaciousness of the landscape we are constantly being packed into vans, dressing-rooms, kitchens, dormitories; and the multifarious activities of the production—publicity, accounting, cooking, line-learning, recording, prop-making, light-plotting, besides the necessary activities of ordinary living, such as gambling, conversation, music and song—all have to be carried on in only two rooms. Even allowing for the general homogeneity of our particular company before we begin in that we are all from universities and training colleges it is still surprising that we manage to live fairly harmoniously under such stressful conditions. Current ethological theories of the relation between crowding and aggression would predict an explosion.

What saves us from that is the play, towards which the various social energies are channelled. Perhaps fancifully, I usually feel I can detect an influence exerted by the play on the people involved in it, not just in the sense that the actors continue to play their parts off stage, for the whole company is involved. Obviously, the character of the company is partly dictated by the initial casting, so that the play makes its influence felt there, but beyond and after that, during rehearsal period, a quite close and complex community comes into being, under the forcing-house conditions of intense communal living, and here again I feel that the character of a given play conditions the structure of the group that forms itself to perform it. For instance, in the year we did *Lear* a general atmosphere of intense application and seriousness alternated with bouts of manic exuberance, which perhaps can be associated with the emotional structure of the scene from *Lear* I described earlier. People found themselves pushed back on the ropes, on the frontiers of their personalities in their encounter with that play, and something had to give. *Henry IV* is less concentrated, and more historical and analytic in structure with its widely separated groups of characters pursuing their competing plots, and that year one had the impression that the company was if not centrifugal, at least a congeries of intersecting circles of people, each circle having a separate centre of interest. One felt that some people were living in a different world or acting on different premises from one's own and one could never really get to meet them. I wouldn't care to try this kind of diagnosis on all of our productions, and perhaps the idea amounts to no more than saying that with *Lear* we were frightened of the risk we were taking on and therefore stretched ourselves, whereas with *Henry IV* we were more confident and therefore concentrated less, which in turn comes to no more than a way of saying that we are only amateurs. Whatever the case, living at such close quarters gives one a pretty intimate working knowledge and tolerance of one's fellows, and co-

operating so intensively on a communal enterprise builds up a
delightful camaraderie offering rich material for future nostalgia,
which God forbid.

Yet why should He? Perhaps a miscellany of the scraps and
fragments that the last eight years have lodged in the mind may
serve as well as anything to suggest what it is that makes one
come back for more. There was the anticipation and unfailing
gratification of surprise at breasting the hill above the theatre
and seeing the great arm of the Logan headland, Porthcurno
Bay, and the Minack below. That is a focus, a representative
moment, an image, an icon, an epiphany for the whole fort-
night. The transformation of the Logan cliffs by the late afternoon light also comes to mind. Or, at night, taking a few steps
out of the lighted path backstage and immediately being over-
whelmed by the presence of the landscape, visible only as the
darker darkness of the cliffs and the fading repetition of the surf.
The image of Katharina, exhausted after her wedding journey to
Petruchio's house, leaning against a pillar. The bizarrerie of a
lighting rehearsal in the small hours sending shadows leaping
over the sea. The frightful bus journey home the first year when
we budgeted on a shoestring, and no one had any sleep for two
nights, and everyone was sick. In *The Winter's Tale* the dance of
the country-folk which seemed to grow and develop out of itself
like something living. Miss Cade pushing a lawnmower over a
6-in-wide plank bridge quite indifferent to the gulf beneath her.
Continuing to act in total darkness, then seeing dozens of torches
switched on by the audience one by one and directed on to the
stage during a power failure. Goneril, Regan and Cordelia
wearing respectively appropriate red, black and white PVC macs
during a wet weather performance of *Lear*. A sailmaker's loft in
Penzance. The warm mingling of browns and yellows in the
tavern scenes of *Henry IV*. Staring over the edge of Minack
Rock and yielding to mesmerism by the rise and fall of the swell.
The sleep-walking entrance of all the characters as shadows for
the curtain-call of *A Midsummer Night's Dream*. The sweet and
sad plain-song played over the loudspeakers as the audience

exited after *A Man for All Seasons.* Dismantling the lights on the Saturday morning after the last evening performance.

If one tries to extract any principles from this confused mass of reminiscence and reflection, they might be the following:

(1) Technical—audibility and visibility; the Minack's demands on these qualities can be taxing.

(2) Stylistic—movement, gesture and bearing must adjust to the nature of the space in which they occur.

(3) Interpretive—the presentation of character must be adjusted to the nature of the relationship with the setting and space and with the audience; the best way to secure this is to emphasise ensemble playing and to aim at creating a world of the play.

Expressed so generally, these principles may sound trite. If they do, then that is presumably because they command universal assent, and it then follows that they should be applied. I have tried to work out their application in terms of my own experience above. Other actors will disagree with my conclusions, for they are necessarily conditioned by my experience, which is partial and limited, and by my ability to understand it, which is defective and idiosyncratic. Still, my experiences and conclusions can have their use as simple testimony, which the reader will supplement and reinterpret according to his lights. I wish him luck.

CHAPTER 4

Lighting the Minack Stage   JO PHELPS

T he Minack Theatre is one of the most unusual theatres in
the country, its shape, size, and actual position are quite
unlike any other. Where else could one find a natural
stage backcloth of such beauty and expanse, with no worry about
the cost of lighting it—or, for that matter, storing it when not in
use! The Minack has none of the usual facilities for stage
lighting, such as spot bars, proscenium arch, wings and masking
borders, but it is this very lack that provides the main interest
of the stage and makes the break from conventional lighting
less difficult.

Where there would normally be a dress circle lighting bar or
box, there is a covered box which houses the main stage area
lighting and from which all the sound and theatre lighting is now
controlled. There are also various seemingly providential rock
ledges outside, which are just the right size for a large spotlight.
On the right side of the stage is a very useful bar, hidden from
the audience by a big rock, and from which one can light the
larger part of the stage and the steps leading down to the grass
circle. On stage left is another lighting position which will light
right across the stage, there are various points behind the balustrade and around the covered box, but some of the most unusual
and useful lighting points are under the front row of the audience seats. These points are on the same level as the stage and
can be used for a variety of effects, from a cosy fireside glow to
dramatic spotlighting of a disembodied head. This is the sort of
effect which is extremely difficult to achieve in an ordinary

84

theatre, with problems of hiding the source of light and losing the shadow that inevitably falls from a high-angled spotlight. This multiplicity of potential hanging or standing positions means that often an effect can be translated to the stage as imagined by the lighting designer, without wasting time and lanterns trying to rig up half-a-dozen of them in odd places to do the work of one in the ideal place. Many theatres lend themselves to adaptable staging, but even so, such things as front-of-house lighting points, spot bars, wings, and masking of lights, are of necessity fixed; and it is not often that a lighting designer can virtually create his own theatre. He can at the Minack because it offers so much scope for imaginative lighting.

Audiences no longer regard glimpses of backstage trappings as something rather indecent that should be hidden from view. In most theatres the audience dictates its desires, theatres are built for and around them, often with more consideration for the audience than for the people backstage. But this is one theatre that creates its own audience. The Minack puts everyone on an equal footing—everyone is at the mercy of the elements; audiences arrive with blankets, cushions, sandwiches, thermos flasks, torches, to sit for two or three hours on grass banks or concrete seats, in heat waves or in pouring rain, on nights when 'the floor of heaven is thick inlaid with patines of bright gold', and nights when there is no escape from a chill wind off the sea. Like the rocks on which and out of which it has been made, this theatre is hard, quite uncompromising, but with a beauty of its own.

The concrete of the stage is so receptive to light that any other stage seems dull by comparison. The suggestion of mood by the colour of light used is one of the most rewarding facets of this theatre. The stage seems alive to the light on it. A scene can be dimly lit and the actors still comfortably visible. A 'moonlight' scene can be played in a light that really looks something like moonlight, and indeed, the moon has been known to put in an appearance right on cue—but that is another story. In the Cambridge University Players' production of *As You Like It*, a cold white light on the circle perfectly suggested the wintry forest of Arden, and coloured lighting from the points under the front seats lent a weird atmospheric effect to the horrifying mad scene in The Interluders' *Peer Gynt*.

On the other hand there are slight incongruities such as full 'sunlight' on stage while it is actually raining cats and dogs—an Anath in *The Firstborn* speaking of the drought in Egypt to a forest of umbrellas while the rain trickled down the back of her neck; and Kent in *King Lear* wrapped in a thick cloak amid 'groans of roaring wind and rain', in the brilliant sunshine of a matinée, with the sweat making streaks in his make-up—this sort of thing puts a certain amount of strain on the actors, the technicians, and the imagination of the audience, and it is greatly to the credit of all concerned that these occasions never raise more than a sympathetic murmur from the front of the house.

The usual way to light a play is to start from blackness; while the show is running there is usually a pause of darkness between the dimming of the auditorium lights and the rising of the curtain. At the Minack the matinée shows do not need lighting and most evening performances start in daylight or twilight, depending on which end of the season you happen to be playing, and therefore for the first forty-five minutes of the play, the stage lights only colour the daylight. Then suddenly you realise that the sky is dark, there is just a faint glimmer of sunlight left on the horizon, and the stage lights have taken over completely.

The 'fit-up', the hanging and setting of lights, has to be done in the hours of darkness. So at sundown, or at curtain-down of the previous company, whichever is the later, the next company moves in with its extra lanterns, cables, colours, a great assortment of tools, clothing, sandwiches, and perhaps most important of all, the Electric Kettle! The prospect of working until dawn without this essential contribution to endurance is too horrifying to be contemplated. Throughout the night cables are run, lanterns hung and set, colours cut, and plugging sorted out in the control box. Then at about five-thirty, the black sky becomes blue and gradually light creeps over the theatre and no more work can be done, so everyone thankfully returns to the base camp, has breakfast, and goes to bed. That evening, at about ten o'clock, we set the lighting cue by cue while the actors run around the stage giving a very speeded-up version of the play, just to ensure that they will be in the right light at approximately the right time. The next day, the Monday, is spent tidying odd bits and pieces or sleeping, as necessary, and that evening we have our first public performance.

Sea mist is a hazard that one does not normally come across when setting up for a show, but here everything has to be waterproof. The theatre provides five 1,000 watt area spots and three 500-watt profile spots, all of which are the outdoor variety. In addition to these each company brings whatever extra lanterns it needs for its particular play, bearing in mind the fact that they are very likely to be rained upon at least once during their stay in Cornwall. There are waterproof versions of most types of plugs; they come in gigantic brass form and are about as waterproof as anything can be out on the cliffs. We usually take a large selection of polythene bags to cover the lanterns when not in use, and these have to be firmly anchored against possible 'roaring wind and rain'.

In the covered box at the back of the theatre are all the lighting and sound controls. There are thirty-two circuits around the theatre which can be plugged into any of the twenty-eight dimmers. There are twelve dimmers, or faders, capable of carrying 500–1,000 watts, and they are mounted side by side on a slightly slanted desk. Beside these are two Strand 'Junior 8' boards which each have eight circuits and four dimmers. These Junior 8 boards stand one on top of the other. The operator usually has to sit down in order to work the top board with hands and the bottom one with feet. Some cues also require noses or chins to supplement the usual quota of hands. The individual dimmers can be controlled by either of two master dimmers, dimmers capable of fading in or out a heavier load of lights. These master dimmers are 4 kW short-rated dimmers, and therefore cannot be used to hold a heavy load on check. I think many companies find it easier to work the individual dimmers, as there are always odd lengths of wood lying in the box to act as an extra pair of hands. The stage supply is 60 amps, and there is a little meter which measures the amps being used, with a red line at 58, and this meter is so placed in the box that it can be carefully watched. In scenes using a lot of light the needle may waver at 56, and then everyone has to be warned not to put the kettle on for the actors' interval tea, as this may result in total darkness! This has happened on occasion. . . .

The first thing the lighting designer should do on moving into the Minack Theatre is to make acquaintance with The Fuse. The fuse box is up in the box office at the top of the cliff, a matter of no small concern to the people working in the box office. Five minutes before 'curtain up' we have been worried by a voice over the theatre telephone telling us that the fuse box is 'making funny noises', or that there is 'an odd burning smell in here', or worse still, 'I can't make any of the lights work up here'. These troubles are usually traced to other sources, such as a transistor radio in that lovely queue for tickets, a near-by camper's evening meal, or they have overlooked the light switch. However, on the odd occasion it *is* the fuse.

Once, during an evening performance of *King Lear*, the stage lights suddenly disappeared. The stage manager raced up the stairs to the box office, flung himself at the offending fuse which was smouldering ominously, and tried to wrench it out of the carrier, muttering 'I'll get this out if it kills me'. As he had omitted to switch off the current it was a strong possibility. In the meantime the audience, confronted with darkness, shone their torches on stage, following the action with a concerted movement that would have done credit to the best follow-spot operator. The fuse eventually gave up the ghost, and a successor was appointed. The stage manager was still in one living piece, the team returned to the box and the lights were restored. To give it its due, the old fuse had done good service. It had just decided that enough was enough.

Nowadays lighting at the Minack is safe, provided that a little

West Cornwall Theatre Group's 1960 production of Shakespeare's *The Winter Tale*

Penzance County School for Girls' production of *Iphigenia in Tauris* (by Euripides) 1954

commonsense is used when fitting up, and that everything is kept as dry as possible. Gone are the days when a brave electrician had to go the rounds of the lights, touching each lantern to ensure that anyone in the audience accidentally doing the same thing would not get a shock.

The usual theatre practice of checking the setting of each lantern before every performance is an absolute necessity here: members of the audience may bump into them on their way out from the previous performance; visitors, or matinée audiences— or their offspring—may be intrigued by these seemingly useless pieces of metal; there may have been a high wind during the night; a lamp may have blown; or, if everything has not been adequately protected from the rain, there may be a short-circuit in one of the lamps. This all sounds very gruesome, and very probably you will find that during the entire run nothing at all will go wrong. But there is such a thing as the law of averages, and it is always as well to be prepared for the worst.

I have heard many criticisms, good and bad, of the theatre, but not one complaint; and never have I heard anyone say that they would not work there again, given a quarter of a chance. Come hell and high water—and they do!—the Minack for me will always be one of the most stimulating and rewarding theatres to light.

CHAPTER 5

Sound at the Minack ALAN RUSSELL

S ound in any theatre, whether open-air or not, can be split
into two main divisions:
    1. Words spoken by the actors or actresses.
    2. Any other noise.

These, of course, can subsequently be broken down into
various subdivisions, but before doing that—and attempting
to iron out the problems which they ultimately involve, especially at the Minack—let us first consider what use sound is in a
production.

First and foremost, the actors talk (unless it's a Mime play).
This might seem obvious, but if an audience can't hear the
words, then they are the first to complain about it—and quite
rightly, because it is the words that give the plot. Missing an
occasional word or even a sentence is normally acceptable to the
average audience because the actors, as well as speaking the
lines, can help to reach the audience in many visual ways—with
gesture, movement and reaction.

Apart from the actors speaking the lines of the play, everything else used in a production is visual—wardrobe, make-up,
lighting, properties, sets and visual effects can all be used to enhance a production and frequently do.

Question: 'What is there left?'

Answer: 'Noises Off'—that terrible, hackneyed, hateful phrase
that is used all too often by those who do not realise that they
are talking about the only pure, non-visual effect in a production
and therefore the most difficult. Because it is a pure, non-visual

92

medium, sound tends to get pushed to one side with the words: 'Who can work a tape recorder?' and the inference that it is a job for the technician.

Those who say this could not be further from the object of sound, which is in its own right a work of art, and which therefore needs an artist to handle it correctly. Sound can enhance or mar a production in the same way that any other department can. If not handled sensitively, results can be disastrous.

What to use, when to use, and how much to use will depend on the play, the director and the style of the production.

What to use and when to use it; this is a matter of individual taste. How much to use, although also a matter of individual taste, gives me the opportunity to state the one rule that I apply when doing sound—if in doubt, it is better to have too little rather than too much. Whether you are using a realistic off-stage effect, live or electronic, mood music on tape or a live orchestra, use sparingly. Remember, the good sound man is the man who, when asking the audience after the show what they thought of the sound effects, gets the reply: 'I didn't really notice them.' You could not receive a better answer—it means that what, when and how much, were right.

Sound is essential in any production—sound that the audience is not only able to hear, but also to understand.

Let us now consider sound at the Minack Theatre. First of all —what has the Minack got to offer?

The auditorium seating is very steeply raked and therefore sound coming from either on or off stage has to travel up a very long way to reach the back row. The Minack also has very high rocks on stage right, which, although being very useful for production gimmicks, virtually make live off-stage noises an impossibility. This is not as bad as it might seem at first, because there is another more important reason why live effects should not be used at the Minack—Nature.

One of the great charms of the Minack Theatre is that it is in the open air. Its backcloth is the moving sea which pounds against the rocks, 70 ft below the back of the stage.

Sound at the Minack

What grander setting could you wish to have for any production?

The Minack is a superb combination of Man and Nature together. Nature, being the unpredictable lady that she is, can bring not only sunshine, but also wind, rain, hail, heat, cold and variable humidity. All of these will affect the sound in some way and as there are so many, it is impossible for me to delve into all the various assumed combinations that you can have and how each can be overcome.

One feature of Nature that is worth a brief word, however, is wind. If there is an off-shore wind, the general opinion is that this would carry the actors' voices away from the audience. Likewise, if the wind is coming from the sea, this would help carry the actors' voices towards the audience. This may all seem very logical in theory, but in practice the reverse is true.

An on-shore wind will also bring with it the tremendous roar of the sea pounding the rocks below. This tends to produce a kind of baffle in the ears of the audience which reduces the actors' voices. On the other hand, an off-shore wind doesn't present this baffle, because most of it goes over the heads of the audience and the actors. Thus, the actors are heard more easily. This probably sounds quite a unique phenomenon; but phenomenon or not—it is true.

I stated earlier that live sound effects should not be used at the Minack because of Nature. It is Nature's wind that is the real reason for this statement. A sudden gust of wind or a directional wind change during the play and the actors will automatically adjust as far as projection of the voice is concerned.

Just as the actors adjust, so should the sound effects. This cannot possibly be done by anyone producing an effect in the wings, because their relationship with the actors, although continually changing, is not necessarily changing in the same way as the actors' relationship to the audience, and it is the latter that is important.

This is one of the reasons why the sound equipment in the

Sound at the Minack

Theatre is controlled from the lighting box which is situated in the centre of the auditorium.

Having decided why any sound effect should be electronic, let us now look at the equipment installed in the Theatre. The system is very basic, which is essential when you remember that many different companies are performing at the Minack, and therefore any system that is used must be simple enough and logical enough for any sound man to use and maintain. The more complex the system, the more likely it is to go wrong.

Three storm-proof loudspeakers are installed—one stage right, one stage left and one under the 'table' centre stage. These can be independently switched for either localised or general effects, and are powered from one unit which has three inputs—mike, gram, tape.

The transistorised unit houses all the mixer and power amplifying circuits, and is simply constructed from basic independent printed circuits for which spares are available and easy to fit. The system has been designed to be 'fool-proof' but it also has the advantage of being able to be added to should the production demand it.

The last time I was stage directing at the Minack was for the Interluders' production of *Dr Faustus*, which had a fairly complex sound plot.

For this production, two tape recorders and two personal neck microphones were required, so I also used a four-by-two mixer and pre-amp unit, the outputs of which fed straight into the inputs of the Minack amplifier.

The use of microphones for actors at the Minack has been discussed by many people, but my personal view is that they should not be used on stage as a public address system. These are too complicated to operate efficiently with stand microphones at the front of the stage, and too expensive to use a radio mike on each actor. I have used microphones on actors at the Minack, but these were for supernatural characters in a production where a special slight-echo sound was required. My main objection to full mike systems is that the Minack is a theatre for 'live' productions and the acoustics are good enough for the average actor who is projecting his voice.

Sound at the Minack is not easy—it is a challenge. A challenge well worth taking on.

CHAPTER 6

Company Management   DEREK RITCHIE

W hen the Interluders was founded in 1963 the concept seemed quite simple. We were going to gather together a group of people chosen from the various dramatic societies in Hertfordshire in order to stage a play at the Minack during the summer holidays, to celebrate the Shakespeare Quatercentenary. Right from the beginning I felt that here was an opportunity to be seized and exploited; on the one hand to gather together a company to rehearse and perform a play at a time of year when most dramatic societies have closed down for the summer and at the same time to lay the emphasis equally on the provision of a seaside holiday for the entire family.

The original idea was for a 'one off' production but even before the play was performed it was quite obvious that many people were looking forward to a return the following year and, in fact, the fourth consecutive Interluders' production is now behind us.

In order to secure the smooth running that the migration of a large company demands, the preliminary work is started a full year in advance and thus every person involved remains interested in the project without feeling the necessity of breaking their allegiance to any other society during the remainder of the year.

Over the last four years many excellent suggestions for possible future productions have been made and each year I pin up in the Minack dressing-room a sheet of paper in order that any further additions can easily be made. Several very good ideas for future plays have been made during the week's run each year, for there is no doubt that it is much easier to weigh the relative advantages and disadvantages of the Minack type of production when you are on the spot.

Running neck and neck with the suitability of the play and really an integral part of the same question is my selection of the producer, for obviously the choice of one will certainly limit and possibly determine the choice of the other. The vision and capacity for exploiting the unique situation and facilities which the Minack has to offer are supremely important, for an apparently inferior play will become a memorable production whilst the finest script can be lost completely by a pedestrian and unimaginative approach.

Trying to accommodate a cast of over forty, with possibly another fifteen theatre staff and technicians, their wives, husbands, sweethearts, children and family animals was a task which could have finished the venture long before it began, for I realised that it was quite impossible to make bookings from a distance of 300 miles without being able to see the facilities offered and explain the very real difficulties under which the company had to work. So we spent several week-ends quartering West Cornwall, listing and docketing everyone who offered bed and breakfast, every caravan and camp site, every farm-house which looked as though it might have accommodation and everybody in the vicinity of the Minack itself who we felt might be sympathetic to the project.

Of course, in this area one is off to a good start as an extremely high proportion of people are prepared to put themselves to the very real inconvenience of letting rooms. Inconvenience as far as the Interluders are concerned it certainly is, for we definitely are an awkward lot! We arrive at the latest on Saturday ready to move into the theatre immediately the preceding company have finished their afternoon or evening performance. We cannot cope with a Sunday to Sunday booking like any respectable holiday-maker. If some very well-meaning landlady has organised matters so that her guests come from Saturday to Saturday then we are still awkward because we cannot really leave until the following Sunday at the very earliest. Then, we want an evening meal certainly no later than half past six and we are unlikely to be back from the theatre much before midnight. Furthermore, the technicians will probably be working right through the night on both Saturdays setting up and striking and the company will try and organise a party towards the end of the week to ruin another evening. This will undoubtedly mean that any attempt to gather the household together for breakfast at any civilised hour is doomed to failure from the start. And then baby sitters have to be found.

In spite of all the difficulties the list grew steadily and the map showed a trail of pins starting within a hundred yards or so of the theatre itself and fanning out to Penzance, covering that part of the southern coast like a hedgehog and stretching in many cases up into the heart of the country above.

Here I really must pay the warmest possible tribute to the way in which we have been looked after. The hospitality has been unstinted and the difference not only to the cast but also to the technical staff who all have a very real job of work to do means that it is a holiday as well.

One thing emerged from the start: practically no one wants hotel accommodation and I cannot remember, in fact, having booked even one in the four years. Possibly this is because, again, no one chooses the towns or even the villages to stay in if a hamlet or isolated cottage or farm-house can be found instead.

Practically every person I visited told me that a firm booking would have to be made by Christmas, or very soon after, and obviously the prospective members of the company themselves would need to make their holiday arrangements by this time also. This fixes the vital necessity of an audition with casting and apportionment of other jobs during the early winter. This has enabled many families to go back year after year to the same place, if they wish, and I am still amazed but very happy to see that so many landladies still welcome us after putting up with our idiosyncrasies for four years.

Company Management

Many people book either for the week before the show or the week following the show as well, and I am afraid that sometimes it becomes unavoidable to move some people into other accommodation for the second week. Partly, this is due to travelling difficulties. Some of our younger members do not possess their own transport and would find the cost of arranging this for themselves prohibitive. I have always managed to find sufficient places in the cars travelling to Cornwall for anyone who needs this, and to batten on the generosity of people when we arrive to see that the carless are not stranded by themselves in a farmhouse three miles from any civilisation. Transport is obviously vital in the evenings to get everybody to the theatre on time and back home again when the show is over. So far there have never been any accidents, but I always keep my fingers crossed.

Transport always has to be arranged for the sets, lighting equipment, sound equipment with loudspeakers, costumes and properties. Scenery, if used at all, is of course very rudimentary, but we had to transport the massive gates for *Tiger at the Gates* in 1966, and the following year the production of *Dr Faustus* called for a lift built at the back of the stage against the cliff face to bring the characters out of Hell and drop them back again when the script demanded it. Tubular steel scaffolding, a strong platform, counter weights and pulleys stout enough to take the fear of the ascent out of the hearts of the characters who needed to use the lift, is a good enough load on its own for any shooting brake.

I know we make many of our own difficulties ourselves, for by insisting on large casts and period plays if possible, so that we can present a colourful and varied spectacle, we have to transport between fifty and a hundred costumes. The Grecian costumes for *Tiger at the Gates* packed very small, Shakespearean costumes bulk somewhat larger, but the packing and transport of the costumes for *Peer Gynt* in 1965 and *Dr Faustus* in 1967, which included elaborate crowns, masks, hats and wigs, added enormously to our problems. It isn't so much the weight that is the problem, for many of the special items have to be

100

packed carefully and separately, it is the resulting cubic space that becomes fantastic.

The commercial hiring of costumes is an expense we cannot really envisage as we would need these for at least a month— two weeks for our dress rehearsals and at least a further two weeks for the show and the period before and after until the costumes could be returned. Thus, nearly everything is now made in the Interluders' wardrobe, designed and produced by a small group of very dedicated helpers whose skill has contributed so much to the success of our productions.

We have, by now, the nucleus of a useful collection of costumes and on occasions the company's income can be augmented, even if only modestly, by charging a small sum for the loan of these to other companies.

The transportation of the sound equipment will fill another car. All sound effects, incidental music, announcements, etc., are fed on to tape and for a complicated show two tape recorders are used; in case of accidents a third is always carried and is ready as a stand-by for immediate use. Always two, generally three, and sometimes four, loudspeakers of adequate size will also be needed around the stage. Often we can use the Minack's own speakers for these are well sited and able to cope with the volume of sound necessary, but for complicated plots and special effects additional speakers are always needed.

My sound engineers have built an amplifier large enough to produce the level of sound needed with a control unit and mixing facilities to cope with all eventualities, whilst of course several hundred yards of cable runs and leads will also be required, again with adequate spare in case of accidents. In addition to this we always augment the Minack inter-com system with an additional microphone and loudspeaker relay so that not only is every major part of the theatre in telephone communication with every other, but also each can hear what is going on on stage at that time, and furthermore the stage director can superimpose on the latter system all calls, cast announcements, and in fact anything that requires theatre-wide distribution.

Even in the best organised theatres things occasionally go wrong, and in one performance of *Dr Faustus* the lift stuck. Within a couple of seconds the stage director had sensed the position from the control box, checked with the lift operators, informed all the technical staff of the danger, issued his orders warning everyone to expect the unexpected, arranged for all spare lights to be trained on alternative entrances, and when Mephistophilis walked up the central stairway instead of rising in the lift he emerged straight into a pool of light, as if it was the most natural thing in the world. The stage director would, of course, say that it was, but without him and without his complete communications equipment I dread to think what might have happened.

The Minack provides a fairly comprehensive lighting scheme, but there always seems to be something extra to take. Producers generally fear the complete collapse of the artistic and dramatic merits of the play unless the weird and wonderful is obtainable, bless them! Each year we have transported a gigantic 2 kW follow spot, and there, in effect, goes all the spare room in yet another car. Of course, we really want our own lorry fitted out to carry all our equipment, but the cost for one show a year would make such a purchase quite uneconomical and so I prefer to keep everything under my eyes if at all possible. The bogey of lightning strikes, mis-deliveries or delays is always enough to frighten me to death unless somebody is brave enough to want to travel with the equipment.

The total effect is that practically everything we take down has to be brought back, for little is expendable. Actually, I try and leave behind the small amount of scenery we do take, and donate to the theatre any timber, etc., which may be worth keeping and pile the remainder on our Saturday night bonfire on the rocks below the theatre, which disposes of the week's rubbish. This clearance of the theatre is a matter about which I hold very strong views and I insist that before we quit on the Saturday night everything is clear, clean and tidy. Moving in to start work at midnight is bad enough at the best of times, but

102

it is made infinitely worse if you have to start off by wasting three-quarters of an hour clearing the dressing-rooms through following somebody else's bibulous last-night party. After all, it does not take very long if everybody has a job and carries it out conscientiously; and if the last performance is on the Saturday afternoon then any supplementary lighting equipment can generally be removed even before the performance.

Publicity seems to go on for practically the entire year. This comprises not only the publicity for the forthcoming show itself but general information about the company and also news of the theatre. A tremendous number of people who are not in the least theatrically minded never fail to have their imagination fired by the story of an open-air theatre hewn out of the cliff face and with only the sea, the path of the moon across the water, and the distant flashes of the lighthouse as a back drop. Two or three general interest stories go out every season and *Amateur Stage, Hertfordshire Topic* as well as the local newspapers and several club and dramatic society magazines have already carried the story. Whilst I fully realise that specific publicity for our company and the show itself is necessary and, indeed, vital, I hold very strongly to the view that everything possible should be done to foster a love of the theatre in people's minds, for this can then be directed towards the Minack in particular and so the nucleus of a regular audience can be built up, which will benefit all companies alike rather than one small group in particular.

General publicity covering the programme for the entire season is, of course, dealt with by the theatre itself and their yellow leaflets can always be seen over a very wide area. During early spring I try and cover the nation-wide organisations— County Women's Institutes, county drama advisers, schools, university groups and so on but, of course, publicity in the Cornish area must be left until the week before the show. There is a gentleman's agreement amongst the various groups, which is unfortunately not always honoured as strictly as I would like, that no publicity in the Cornish area will be done until at least the middle of the week prior to the playing dates and that no publicity whatever in the very west of Cornwall, say within 15 miles radius of the theatre, shall be done until the day of the previous company's last performance, which is normally the Saturday. Nothing is more galling than to find in the middle of one's own performances that the posters within a mile or so of the theatre have already been overlaid with the next company's posters.

We have reduced the different types of publicity material we carry to two and each year about 10,000 copies of our standard information leaflets are printed. The layout of this has remained unchanged over the four years and gives details not only about the play, the author and the company, but also a short description of the theatre, how it can best be approached, ticket arrangements and so on, all in a space a little larger than an ordinary quarto sheet. The regular theatregoers will not, of course, read the leaflet in detail each time but by now will recognise the format, whilst we know that the additional information is always of interest and use to newcomers to the area. In fact, it has been known for people to arrive at the Minack led by our leaflet in order to see the play that followed ours. It must prove something.

Circularisation of these leaflets nationally will, as I have said before, already have taken place before our publicity team leaves for Cornwall early on Wednesday morning of the week before we open. They will carry the balance, about 6,000 of the leaflets and up to fifty individually produced and hand-painted double crown or larger posters for special display. By Wednesday night Newquay and Truro and the country in between will have been covered. Thursday covers Redruth and Falmouth; Friday, Helston, the Lizard area and up to St Ives; Saturday, St Ives itself, Penzance and the area to the west, whilst the area immediately around the theatre can be filled in on Sunday morning, if necessary. To put it like that sounds relatively simple, but it takes two people working at least twelve hours a day virtually non-stop for the first three days, and four or even six can, with advantage, be deployed on the Saturday.

Company Management

Basically the coverage is quite simple, or at least it is simple on paper and it is only when one begins to transform the theory into practice that the magnitude of the task becomes obvious. Everywhere that people gather either a leaflet or a poster should be seen. In the larger towns, the information bureaux, museums, libraries, art galleries, local theatres or dramatic companies, every possible hotel and boarding house, bus stations, every shop in the town centre and in the sub-centre which will co-operate, all receive one or more leaflets and, if it can be displayed to advantage, a poster.

Certain classes of shop are more important than others. Art galleries, potteries, gift shops and every type which attracts the tourist and holiday maker should receive special attention and it is far better to offer to display the poster even if it does take a few more minutes rather than to hand it over with no certainty that it will be shown to advantage. My publicity team always carry Sellotape, drawing pins and glue with them for this purpose.

In each town, also, one or more newsagent can usually be persuaded to distribute leaflets with the paper round, whilst on the outskirts of the town all camping and caravan sites must be covered. This is an ever-growing potential audience which I do not feel is tapped sufficiently. Continual enquiries from the established camp sites are received and more should be done to see that details of all local amenities are given to the camp offices. Even my hardened publicity team never fails to be impressed by the continual interest of the hotel receptionists, shop-keepers, caravan site officers and the many others who accept a leaflet, not as just another piece of paper, but with genuine interest to see for themselves what will be on at the the theatre and with a very ready desire to help to publicise the plays to their customers.

Then, of course, a network of poster sites has been built up with the co-operation of helpful farmers who put their barn doors readily at our disposal and the many road-side house-holders who are happy for us to disfigure their garages.

To my mind, one of the most important rules is never to fly post. Permission should always be obtained for a new site and the one used previously should, of course, be checked. Close around the theatre there are always certain recognised sites which are in constant use, but if you poster the side of somebody's house without asking him, you will certainly make an enemy, and if you do ask him it's an even chance that you may gain another member of the audience.

Several large car parks will also repay attention. There is, of course, the Porthcurno car park itself at the bottom of the hill below the theatre, but the two most useful always seem to be the large new car park at St Ives and the one almost on the beach facing St Michael's Mount. A half an hour spent at a fast trot up and down the lines of parked cars gets rid of an amazing number of leaflets, but remember to ask the car park attendant first.

Of course we have our special friends—the landlords at the 'Logan Rock' and 'The Old Success' dispose of the most fantastic number of leaflets and although the temptation on Friday evening to throw two or three packets of leaflets over Land's End may be fairly great the publicity team always seem to finish up empty-handed. In 1966 they had ten posters to display and at our post-show discussion told me that they thought they could manage another four, so the following year I gave them fifty and every one went up, and what is more, displayed to advantage. That must prove something, too!

Two special places receive very individual treatment; the Information Centre in Penzance has a special display board and similar but larger boards are erected at Porthcurno at the head of the beach path. These have pictures of the theatre, cast and previous productions with excerpts from the press criticism. The local papers—both in Cornwall and Hertfordshire—always print a criticism of the plays and I feel that we have been very fortunate in the last two years to receive a notice from the regional drama critic of *The Guardian*.

May I be pardoned for saying that the best publicity in the

When the wind blows east of south, the roar of waves pounding on the Minack is powerful competition for actors' voices. Fortunately the prevailing wind is south-west

In this pre-1932 photograph, the only hint of what is to come is the faint zigzag path (just above and to the right of the Minack rock, on the far left of the picture)

Another scene from *Ondine*, performed by the Priory Players

theatrical world is the quality of the merchandise itself; the appeal of the theatre, the overall standard of presentation of the plays which appear there, all matter to some extent, but more important than anything is the quality of one's own presentation.

CHAPTER 7

A Seat at the Minack

FRANK RUHRMUND

I shivered in the rain. The corners of my programme curled with the cold. Pulling my cap lower, my oilskin higher, until only my nose was exposed to the elements, I tried to concentrate upon what was happening on stage. It was raining there too. The players, bent bravely against the wild wind that wrapped their costumes wetly around them, slip-slapped through the pools spreading across the stage, their sandals awash. An angry sea roared and railed at the rocks below, threatening to drown us all. I tasted salt in the rain.

I could hear little above the racket made by the rampaging wind and sea. Like fish in a pond, the players swam open-mouthed around the stage, chasing words which the wind whipped from their tongues and tore to shreds, flinging the beaten remains to the dark. I could not see much either. Perhaps it would be more accurate to say that I could see too much; the rain spattered my glasses and distorted my vision until I was seeing two of everything. When this happened my handkerchief came into use as a windscreen wiper, until that too was saturated. I tried watching without my glasses. A myopic water rat, I squatted and peered at the gesticulating, gyrating, silent shapes below me.

Three figures rose directly in front of me, they looked huge against the black night and blotted out the little I could see. Mumbling and grumbling to themselves they walked away and

'Enter Caliban', from the woodcut design for the first Minack production
The Tempest, 1932, by kind permission of Hilda M. Quick

G*

up the steps. The three wise men, I thought; only one was a woman. It would be dry and warm where they were going, and I envied them their sense. For the umpteenth time I wondered why I had come 'in such a night as this', and more, why I bothered to stay. I knew I would stick it out, I had done so before, but why?

There was no hope of the weather improving, and I could lay no claim to courage, my perseverance stemmed only from a deep-rooted stinginess. I had paid for my seat, and, come what may, I was determined to have full value for my money. There was too a certain admiration for the cast, impossible to deny. If they, poor wet souls, could stick it out, then I could. It was as simple and stupid as that.

I looked around at the others, the rows of hunched, huddled figures, who were also sticking it out. Were they like me, simply mean, or was something else keeping them there? And why had they come? Which led me once again into questioning my own motives for being there. That wet windy night was the only free one I had in that particular week, which was as good a reason as any, I suppose. But I could have stayed at home, watched television, done a thousand other things. Why, then, had I come? Why, in fact, do I go to the Minack as often as I do? In the beginning there was the novelty, then there was the magic (disregarding the exaggerated sentiment that the Minack evokes insome people, there *is* magic), but both have faded with familiarity; what induces me to go week after week in season after season?

I am often told I am lucky to live in Cornwall, and I believe I am; but life here also has its disadvantages, and the greatest by far, for me anyway, is the lack of theatre. There is no professional theatre in the county, and apart from the occasional one-night stands performed by touring companies, Cornwall for nine months of the year is a theatrical desert. So for the remaining three months, the eleven or twelve weeks of the summer season of plays presented there, the Minack becomes an oasis where those thirsty for theatre gather to drink their fill.

A Seat at the Minack

It is tempting, as I know only too well, to over-indulge, to become intoxicated with quantity rather than quality. The knowledge that it is my ration for the year makes me want to see everything that is staged there, whether good, bad, or indifferent, and has developed my awful acquisitive instinct to such an extent that I now collect Minack plays, as I once collected cigarette cards. Like most humans, I am a creature of habit, and the Minack has become a habit that I cannot break, that I have no wish to break. A summer without it would no longer seem complete.

All of which sums up my reasons for being a Minack fan, and possibly accounts also for the presence of most local supporters, but what of 'the foreigners'? From its modest beginnings, with its enthusiastic but numerically small audiences, the Minack now attracts some 20,000 people a year, the majority of whom are visitors to the county. People without whom audiences at the Minack would remain rather thin, for the percentage of local supporters is sadly small. Among the visitors are many who have become regular Minack-goers, what is it then that draws them there? Mere curiosity at first, I suspect, and the prospect of seeing a play performed in such novel surroundings.

Sooner or later, when discussing all the good things Cornwall has to offer the summer visitor, the question arises, 'We are thinking of taking a trip to the Minack Theatre, is it worth it?' Which is met with an unequivocal, 'Yes'. A reply that is followed invariably by, 'What's it like there?' The answer to which does not spring to mind quite so easily. Granted half a day to think about it, and a couple of hours to expound upon it, one might begin to give a reasoned reply, but the spur of the moment elicits nothing better than a stumbling mumble about rocks, sea, scenery, and ends with the not very original suggestion that the best thing the curious traveller can do is to go and see for himself. Assuming that the curious traveller takes kindly to the suggestion, what does he find, what is it like there, and what induces him to come again?

Apart from the qualities of the particular play and players on view, the success of any visit to any theatre depends very much upon the prevailing physical and psychological state of the visitor. A pleasant journey to the theatre, a comfortable seat in a good position, the right company, the memory or promise of an excellent meal, all assist the 'tuning-in' process, until one is receptive enough to be agreeably entertained by almost anything. But at the Minack there is the hazard of the weather. In any producer's prayer at this theatre, the plea for fine weather must surely rate top priority. Each year, when the programme of plays for the forthcoming season is announced, I marvel at the management's optimism and courage. Even to think that an English summer will allow some eleven or twelve plays to be performed in the open air is madness. The suprising thing, of course, is that they are performed, and with an astonishingly low cancellation rate: an average of only four or five performances per season. Given favourable weather conditions the success of a Minack visit is more than half assured, but even so, there are other hazards to be reckoned with.

Assuming that one survives the journey down the cliff, and arrives safely, there comes the problem of where to sit; down front or up back; left, right, or centre; on grass or on concrete. For one I know there is no problem of choice, 'I like to sit on the extreme right, near the back, so that I can see the Lizard lighthouse'! For another, who must have surely mis-spent his youth at the old Windmill Theatre, 'I always sit in the front row where I can see the girls better.' And yet another, who likes the seat that bears the name of the play in which she once played a part many years ago. 'I never feel happy anywhere else.' But for most people it is a problem. A seat close to the stage promises a good view of the performance and an excellent chance of hearing all that is spoken, but it limits the outlook. If the attention wanders from the performance there is nowhere for it to go, whereas in the upper rows of the auditorium one is so far removed from the stage that, unless the performers are in good voice and the elements kind, little or nothing will be heard, but a grand view of the sea and all that moves upon it is there to arrest the drifting concentration. The solution to the problem would appear to lie in compromise, a seat neat the centre, but too many people have already discovered this, with the result that there the congestion is greatest. Then should it be to left or right of centre? All things considered it remains very much a case of 'You pays your money, you takes your choice.'

I have been asked at times if I have a favourite seat, and if so, where? That I have a favourite is no secret, but its exact location is. As it is, I manage to secure it for myself in about one visit out of every three; if I told the world I would forego all hope of ever getting it again. People, I have learned to my cost, are like that. The problem of a choice of seats rests on the assumption that there *is* a choice. Such is the popularity of the Minack now that most people are glad to take a seat wherever they can get one. To some extent it has become a case of 'You pays your money, you *grabs* your choice.'

There was a time, and not so very long ago, when a trip to the Minack was quite a leisurely affair. I have spent many a day in the sun and sea at Porthcurno, or nearby Pednevounder or Porth Chapel, and decided casually, almost absentmindedly, when sun and sea have grown cold, to complete a pleasant day by dropping in at the Minack (after a pint, perhaps, at the 'Logan Rock') before returning home; but the theatre with its growing popularity, its large audiences, their increasing demands, and the administration necessary to meet these demands, has lost much of its original air of spontaneity and casual charm, and with it some of the fun. Or am I now wallowing in exaggerated sentimentality? I do not know. I do know that it is still possible to recapture something of this atmosphere during the first week or two of a season, possibly in the last week also, and certainly on those nights when the weather is foul and sensible folk stay at home.

I have said that granted favourable weather conditions the success of a visit to the Minack is more than half assured. Allowing then that one has fine weather and acquires a seat that pleases, success would seem to be fully assured; but it is not as straightforward as that. There is still the wildlife to be considered. It is an entomologist's paradise, for insects love the Minack. I know nothing of the habits of earwigs, but if they congregate prior to hibernating or migrating, or whatever it is they do together, then the Minack is their No. 1 rendezvous, and I manage somehow to attract the attention of a whole herd of them, which gallops all over me each time I am there. Then there are the spiders, all makes of them, the slugs, the snails, the beetles and the midges; some provide an added interest, sometimes a welcome diversion, and always entertainment. The moths, unable to resist the lure of the lights, trace their black and silver flight patterns above and around the players, casting long looming shadows out of all proportion to their size; the bats zoom suddenly out of nowhere and spin, roll and loop their crazy, neck-or-nothing way back to it, leaving the night empty, as if they had never been; and the birds, the jackdaws chattering as they hurry through the twilight to their holes in the cliffs, and the seagulls scavenging, screaming and wheeling around the stern of a fishing boat ploughing a familiar path towards Mousehole or Newlyn; the same birds that will later, when all is dark and still, and for no obvious reason, burst suddenly into angry voice, drowning momentarily all human sound; the black-coated cormorants bobbing to the rhythm of the sea, their periscope necks up, their eyes down searching the depths, waiting for the tell-tale flash of their scaly prey.

But now, at last seated comfortably, with the sun in a cloudless sky, or the moon and stars above, and immune to, or at least prepared for possible attack, from any one of a number of varieties of wild creature, one is ready to enjoy the performance. But no, not yet, not quite; there is still the question of food to be considered, and a considerable question it is, too! The picnic—perhaps feast would be a better word—has become as much a part of the Minack tradition as concern for the weather, choice of seat, and the wildlife. There can be no other theatre in which so much food is consumed in so short a time. Some years ago I called at a friend's house, to find his wife busy in the kitchen, her table laden with pies, sandwiches, cakes, fruit, tin-foil and paper bags. I swear there was enough food on that table to have enabled the family to have withstood a siege of six months, but she explained that they were going to the Minack that night, and she thought she had better prepare a snack.

I must confess I practised the picnic habit myself for a long time until a couple of seasons ago when my Minack-going coincided with a determined attempt to lose weight and I resolved to give up all superfluous food. A resolution I have kept, despite having been dangerously close to breaking point on more than one occasion.

My most severe test came in the third week of my 'fast', when a large group of young people from the far end of Cornwall came to the Minack and occupied a row of seats near me. They had an excellent catering officer for they arrived with huge boxes of provisions, all efficiently labelled, and with flasks of coffee the size of oil-drums. They began with soup which appeared to be piping hot, followed by a few gallons of coffee, which I was able to watch with an amused, academic interest only. I knew they had travelled a considerable distance to get there and was willing to excuse their prodigality; and neither soup nor coffee held the slightest temptation for me, anyway. But during the interval they really put me on the rack. They opened the biggest box of all and produced a pasty, a steaming hot pasty, for each person. It was diabolical. For a Cornishman it was both physical and mental torture to sit and smell and see pasties being eaten without participating. I stuck it for as long as I could, then fled to the car park to forget.

Spartan-like I am now able to sit at the Minack and observe objectively, and self-righteously too, no doubt, the eating habits of others. The picnic people, if one can call them that, can be placed into one of three wide categories: those who eat before the performance begins, those who restrain themselves until the interval, and those who begin eating the moment they arrive and carry on eating until they leave. Those who eat prior to the performance may be people who have travelled some distance to get to the theatre, or who have spent the day on the beach and complete it by a visit to the Minack. In either case their hunger and the need to satisfy it is understandable. Those who indulge during the interval do so, I believe, not because of any great urge for food, but simply out of habit. There is an interval and one must do something. As for the compulsive, perpetual eaters, in all probability they eat like this wherever they go. It can be annoying to sit close to one of this clan, for as well as the sound of sea, wind, and gulls, one has the crackle of food being unwrapped and the crunch of jaws to contend with.

You, of course, may not fit into any of these categories, and may have no wish at all to join in the general junketing, but you might well fancy a drink in the interval, in which case be warned, the Minack is 'dry'. Coffee can be obtained from a vending machine at the back of the auditorium, but there is always a long queue, and it would be wiser to take your own.

Most of the comments I have made so far relate to the normal evening performances at the Minack. I have been to no more than half a dozen afternoon performances and have found them disappointing. It is even more difficult to concentrate in daylight, which relentlessly reveals all, dispels illusion completely, and makes the suspension of disbelief wellnigh impossible. And then there is the occasional 'late, late show'. These have become known as 'midnight matinées'; with typical British absurdity they do not start, of course, at midnight, but more usually at 10 p.m. There is no denying that there is a curious excitement to be had in being on the cliffs at such a time, and I have enjoyed thoroughly the few late performances I have seen, but each time I have journeyed homeward saying to myself, 'This is the last time, they are too late, and just not worth the effort.' I suspect that most companies agree with me, for they are presented less frequently than before.

The time has come, I think, to state quite categorically: 'Minack, with all thy faults, I love thee still.' For despite my carping, the Minack has an undeniable, undefinable attraction. It has a long string of successes to its credit, and continues to give pleasure, season after season, to a tremendous number of people. In view of the thousand and one things that can go wrong, the many ungovernable factors peculiar to the Minack that can make or mar a production there, it is remarkable that it functions as well as it does.

I remember nights when there really has been magic at the Minack. When a whole production has held me from start to finish. When parts of another have gripped and dragged me willingly into another world. When an individual performance has moved me. The awful, the boring, the wet and cold nights, and the nights when everything went wrong, have vanished, and only a kaleidoscope of happy memories revolving in a spectrum of fun remain. Apart from the memorable productions and performances, there are numerous isolated incidents, recalled with great pleasure, that must fit somewhere into the merry jigsaw of the Minack's attraction. There was the night an ocean liner came in close to the shore and even the players stopped to look. The night a long line of French students sat following the text of an Irish play performed by English actors. The cold windy night a scantily-dressed couple bravely took their seat and we placed bets on how long they would stay. Another wind-ridden night when an actor's hat blew off as he was making his exit, and a rich, raw 'Damn!' rattled loud and clear around the auditorium. And the nights when the air is still, when the stars are in both sky and sea, and the man in the moon paints the rocks white and warms the world, and 'we take no note of time'.

Finally, for your trip to the Minack, may I offer this advice. Choose your day carefully, but do not be put off by the weather your particular area happens to be receiving. Cornish weather, like most things Cornish, works in a mysterious and wonderful way. It can be raining at Penzance, while it is fine at Porthcurno. Ring the theatre to find out what conditions there are like. On the day, leave early. If you want a choice of seat it is essential to be there at least three-quarters of an hour before the curtain is due to go up. Check the times of performances: they can, and do, vary. Note where you park your car, they all look alike in the dark, and with luck you will be first up the lane and on to the open road, homeward bound, warmly wrapped in the afterglow, the magic of a night at the Minack, already wanting, as I am sure you will be, and planning, as so many have before you— to come again.

APPENDIX

List of Productions

1932 THE TEMPEST
   Local Players

William Shakespeare
   Producer: T. C. Macaulay

1933 TWELFTH NIGHT
   Local Players & Professionals

William Shakespeare
   Producer: E. Peirce

1935 Triple Bill—
   THE PLAY OF THE WEATHER
   Local Players
   GRINGOIRE
   Local Players
   THE JACKDAW OF RHEIMS
   Local Players

John Heywood

Anon.

Richard H. Barham
   Producers: D. Valentine,
   N. Wrigley

1937 ANTONY AND CLEOPATRA
   Local Players

William Shakespeare
   Producer: N. Porter

1939 TRISTAN AND ISOLT
   Warwick Players

John Masefield
   Producer: W. Berssenbrugge,
   under the guidance of
   Violet Vanburgh

   THE COUNT OF MONTE CRISTO
   Warwick Players

Dumas (adapted)
   Producer: W. Berssenbrugge,
   under the guidance of
   Violet Vanburgh

INTERVAL FOR WAR

During which Gainsborough Pictures Ltd used the theatre for the location
of a film—LOVE STORY—Margaret Lockwood—Stewart Grainger

1949 THE TROJAN WOMEN
   Penzance County Grammar
   Schools

Euripides, Tr. *Gilbert Murray*
   Producer: G. M. Tranter

121

List of Productions

1951 TRISTAN OF CORNWALL   *N. Ratcliff*
      Chiefly Cornish Amateur
        Players   *Producer:* N. Ratcliff

1952 EVERYMAN   *Traditional*
      Anon—Cornwall Religious
        Drama Fellowship   *Producer:* F. Hainsselin
      THE NET   *N. Ratcliff*
        Chiefly Cornish Players   *Producer:* N. Ratcliff
      THE TEMPEST   *William Shakespeare*
        Bedford School Dramatic   *Producer:* C. E. Rhodes
        Society   Harrison

1953 THE ALMOND TREE   *Averil Demuth*
      Credo Players   *Producer:* Averil Demuth
      PROPHESY TO THE WIND   *Norman Nicholson*
      Chiefly Cornish Players   *Producer:* F. Collingwood-
                        Selby
      KING LEAR   *William Shakespeare*
      Ardingly College Drama Club   *Producer:* R. Hamilton
      ARTHUR OF BRITAIN   *N. Ratcliff*
      West Cornwall Theatre Group   *Producer:* N. Ratcliff

1954 THOR WITH ANGELS   *Christopher Fry*
      Cornwall Religious Drama
        Fellowship   *Producer:* E. Chapman
      Concert by the
        Mousehole Male Voice Choir
      TOBIAS AND THE ANGEL   *James Bridie*
      West Cornwall Theatre Group   *Producer:* N. Ratcliff
      IPHIGENIA IN TAURIS   *Euripides,* Tr. *Gilbert Murray*
      Penzance County School for   *Producer:* G. M. Tranter
        Girls
      A MIDSUMMER NIGHT'S DREAM   *William Shakespeare*
      Ardingly College Drama Club   *Producer:* R. Hamilton
      BALLETS MINERVA
      in a varied programme   *Director:* E. Gaillard
      NOAH   *Andre Obey,* Tr. *Arthur Wilmurt*
      Stonaford Players   *Producer:* A. K. Boyd

1955 MACBETH   *William Shakespeare*
      West Cornwall Theatre Group   *Producer:* N. Ratcliff
      ST. URSULA   *John Prudhoe*
      Cornwall Religious Drama
        Fellowship

List of Productions

1956 THE FIRSTBORN
    Cornwall Religious Drama
      Fellowship
  JULIUS CAESAR
    West Cornwall Theatre Group
  THE LOGAN ROCK
    Cornwall Opera Group

Christopher Fry

    Producer: C. Murray Andrews
William Shakespeare
    Producer: N. Ratcliff
Inglis Gundry
    Producer: Powell-Lloyd
      Conductor: Marcus Dods

1957 THE BOY WITH A CART
    Cornish Religious Drama
      Fellowship
  THE TAMED FALCON
    West Cornwall Theatre Group
  TWELFTH NIGHT
    Bristol Youth Company

Christopher Fry

    Producer: Averil Demuth
Nora Ratcliff
    Producer: N. Ratcliff
William Shakespeare
    Producer: Denis Raymond

1958 THE MARVELLOUS HISTORY OF
    ST BERNARD
      Cornwall Religious Drama
        Fellowship
  'COME UNTO THESE YELLOW
    SANDS'
    Priory Players Bristol
  THE TAMING OF THE SHREW
    West Cornwall Theatre Group
  KING RICHARD II
    Ardingly College Drama Club
  THE VIRGIN GODDESS
    Bristol Youth Company

Henri Ghéon

    Producer: Averil Demuth

(Triple bill)
    Producer: Barbara MacRae
William Shakespeare
    Producer: N. Ratcliff
William Shakespeare
    Producer: Richard Hamilton
Rudolph Bessier
    Producer: Denis Raymond

1959 NOAH
    Cornwall Religious Drama
      Fellowship
  ANTIGONE
    Stonaford Players
  CAESAR AND CLEOPATRA
    West Cornwall Theatre Group
  KING HENRY IV, part I
    Ardingly College Drama Club
  OTHELLO
    Gloucestershire County Theatre
      Club

André Obey
    Producer: F. Collingwood-
      Selby
Jean Anouilh
    Producer: A. K. Boyd
G. Bernard Shaw
    Producer: Mary Gealer
William Shakespeare
    Producer: Richard Hamilton
William Shakespeare
  Producers: W. Joseph Cox,
    Elizabeth Jupp

1960 THE COMEDIAN
    Cornwall Religious Drama
      Fellowship

Henri Ghéon

    Producer: Doris Wernhard

123

List of Productions

KING LEAR *William Shakespeare*
Lincoln College Players Oxford *Producer:* D. Goldberg
THE WINTER'S TALE *William Shakespeare*
West Cornwall Theatre Group *Producer:* F. Bechhofer
THE LADY'S NOT FOR BURNING *Christopher Fry*
The Playgoers' Theatre Club
Penzance *Producer:* Averil Demuth

1960 A PHOENIX TOO FREQUENT *Christopher Fry*
Priory Players Bristol *Producer:* Barbara MacRae
BALLETS MINERVA *Repertoire*
Minerva Productions London *Producer:* Edward Gaillard
THE TAMING OF THE SHREW *William Shakespeare*
Cambridge University Players *Producer:* F. Bechhofer

1961 MARY STUART *Schiller*
West Cornwall Theatre Group *Producer:* J. Bryant
BALLETS MINERVA *Repertoire*
Minerva Productions London *Producer:* Edward Gaillard
MEASURE FOR MEASURE *William Shakespeare*
Cambridge University Players *Producer:* F. Bechhofer
LOVE'S LABOUR'S LOST *William Shakespeare*
Ardingly College Drama Club *Producer:* R. Hamilton

1962 BALLETS MINERVA *Repertoire*
Minerva Productions London *Producer:* Edward Gaillard
A PENNY FOR A SONG *John Whiting*
The Buskins, Oxford *Producer:* Mark Cullingham
ST JOAN *George Bernard Shaw*
Nottingham University
Theatre Co. *Producer:* John Miller
HAMLET *William Shakespeare*
West Cornwall Theatre Group *Producer:* John Bryant
BEAUTY AND THE BEAST *Nicholas Stuart Gray*
Playgoers' Theatre Club
Penzance *Producer:* Averil Demuth
THE YOUNG ELIZABETH *Dowling and Letton*
Penzance Young Playgoers *Producer:* Doris Wernhard
THE RAPE OF THE BELT *Benn W. Levy*
Priory Players, Bristol *Director:* Barbara MacRae
AS YOU LIKE IT *William Shakespeare*
Cambridge University Players *Director:* Frank Bechhofer
ELEKTRA *Sophocles* (new trans.)
Studio Theatre Club, Salisbury *Producer:* David Gower
COMUS—A MASQUE *John Milton*
Guildhall School of Music &
Drama *Producer:* Daphne Kershaw

124

List of Productions

1963 BALLETS MINERVA | *Repertoire*
Balmin Productions Ltd | *Director:* Edward Gaillard
ROMEO AND JULIET | *William Shakespeare*
Oxford University Players | *Director:* Mark Cullingham
THE FIRSTBORN | *Christopher Fry*
West Cornwall Theatre Group | *Producer:* John Bryant
ADVENTURE STORY | *Terence Rattigan*
Playgoers' Theatre Club,
Penzance | *Producer:* Averil Demuth
THE TEMPEST | *William Shakespeare*
Shakespeare Players | *Director:* Jean-Pierre Voos
A MIDSUMMER NIGHT'S DREAM | *William Shakespeare*
Cambridge University Players | *Director:* Frank Bechhofer
CYMBELINE | *William Shakespeare*
Studio Theatre Club, Salisbury | *Producer:* Tony Neale
Concert by the
Mousehole Male Voice Choir | *Conductor:* Sampson Hosking

1964 TAMBURLAINE THE GREAT (Pt I) | *Christopher Marlowe*
The Fletcher Players,
Cambridge | *Producer:* John Hope-Mason
LADIES' DAY | *Aristophanes*
Oxford University Players | *Director:* Graham Harley
KING LEAR | *William Shakespeare*
Nottingham University
Dramatic Society | *Director:* Jay Williams
TWELFTH NIGHT | *William Shakespeare*
West Cornwall Theatre Group | *Producer:* John Bryant
THE MERCHANT OF VENICE .... *William Shakespeare*
The Interluders, Hertford | *Producer:* Derek Forbes
DARK OF THE MOON | *Richardson and Berney*
Leicester Drama Society | *Producer:* Geoffrey Sharp
MUCH ADO ABOUT NOTHING | *William Shakespeare*
Playgoers' Theatre Club,
Penzance | *Producer:* Averil Demuth
ONDINE | *Jean Giraudoux*
The Priory Players | *Producer:* Barbara MacRae
THE WINTER'S TALE | *William Shakespeare*
Cambridge University Players | *Director:* Frank Bechhofer
MACBETH | *William Shakespeare*
The Shakespeare Players | *Director:* Hugh Morrison
A MAN FOR ALL SEASONS | *Robert Bolt*
Aldenham School Dramatic
Society | *Producer:* Richard Jones

1965 AS YOU LIKE IT | *William Shakespeare*
Trinity Players, Oxford | *Producer:* Derek Nicholls

125

List of Productions

TOAD OF TOAD HALL   *Kenneth Graham*, adapted by
  The Fletcher Players,   *A. A. Milne*
  Cambridge   *Director:* Simon Richardson
ALICE IN WONDERLAND   *Lewis Carroll*
  University & Christ Church   *Producer:* Adrian Benjamin
  Dramatic Societies, Oxford
CORIOLANUS   *William Shakespeare*
  The Prospice Players   *Producer:* T. Martin
AMPHYTRION   *John Dryden*
  Leicester Drama Society   *Producer:* Geoffrey Sharp
A MIDSUMMER NIGHT'S DREAM   *William Shakespeare*
  West Cornwall Theatre Group   *Producer:* John Bryant
PEER GYNT   *Henrik Ibsen*
  The Interluders, Hertford   *Producer:* Barbara David
COCK-A-DOODLE DANDY   *Sean O'Casey*
  Playgoers' Theatre Club,
  Penzance   *Producer:* Frank Ruhrmund
KING LEAR   *William Shakespeare*
  Cambridge University Players   *Producer:* Frank Bechhofer
THE DEVIL'S DISCIPLE   *George Bernard Shaw*
  Mountview Theatre Club   *Director:* Peter Scott-Smith
THE TAMING OF THE SHREW   *William Shakespeare*
  Aldenham School Dramatic
  Society   *Producer:* Arthur Hearnden

1966 THE RELAPSE   *Sir John Vanbrugh*
  The Fletcher Players,
  Cambridge   *Producer:* Peter Watson
TEAHOUSE OF THE AUGUST MOON   *John Patrick*
  Southampton University
  Theatre Group   *Producer:* Tony Nicholls
RICHARD II   *William Shakespeare*
  The Oxford Drama Company   *Producer:* Adrian Benjamin
ASSAULT AT ARMS LENGTH   *Alfredo Balducci*
  Playgoers' Theatre Club,
  Penzance   *Producer:* Peter Cox
TOAD OF TOAD HALL   *A. A. Milne*
  Leicester Drama Society   *Producer:* John Northam
THE RIVALS   *R. B. Sheridan*
  West Cornwall Theatre Group   *Producer:* Frank Drew
THE MIRACLE WORKER   *William Gibson*
  The Priory Players   *Producer:* Barbara MacRae
TIGER AT THE GATES   *Jean Giraudoux*
  The Interluders, Hertford   *Producer:* Barbara David
HENRY IV (Pt I)   *William Shakespeare*
  Cambridge University Players   *Director:* Frank Bechhofer

WUTHERING HEIGHTS — *Packington and Water*
Liverpool University Dramatic
Society — *Producer:* Stephen Holden

1967 TWELFTH NIGHT — *William Shakespeare*
The Fletcher Players,
Cambridge — *Producer:* Jeremy Davies
MEASURE FOR MEASURE — *William Shakespeare*
Trinity Players, Oxford — *Producer:* Rod Griffin
THE MURDER OF MARIA MARTEN — *Brian J. Burton*
The Comedy Club — *Producer:* Denys Edwards
THE LARK — *Jean Anouilh*
Playgoers' Theatre Club,
Penzance — *Producer:* Ronald Luke
THE HOSTAGE — *Brendan Behan*
Leicester Drama Society — *Producer:* Geoffrey Sharp
THE MERCHANT OF VENICE — *William Shakespeare*
West Cornwall Theatre Group — *Producer:* John Bryant
RING ROUND THE MOON — *Christopher Fry*
The Priory Players — *Producer:* Barbara MacRae
PHAEDRA — *Jean Racine*
The Questors, London — *Director:* Alan Chambers
DR FAUSTUS — *Christopher Marlowe*
The Interluders, Hertford — *Producer:* Robert Ferguson
A MAN FOR ALL SEASONS — *Robert Bolt*
Cambridge University Players — *Director:* Frank Bechhofer
MURDER IN THE CATHEDRAL — *T. S. Eliot*
Kelly College Dramatic Society — *Producer:* Robert Edwards
WEST SIDE STORY — *Leonard Bernstein*
National Association of Boys'
Clubs — *Producer:* Alan Tipton

1968 THE BEGGAR'S OPERA — *John Gay*
Corpus Fletcher Players,
Cambridge — *Producer:* Anthony Harding
THE SHOEMAKER'S HOLIDAY — *Thomas Dekker*
Bristol Old Vic Theatre School — *Director:* Nat Brenner
1066 AND ALL THAT — *Sellar and Yeatman*
Southampton University
Drama Society — *Producer:* Howard Davies
RICHARD II — *William Shakespeare*
Playgoers' Theatre Club
Penzance — *Producer:* John Bryant
THE CRUCIBLE — *Arthur Miller*
Gatehouse Theatre Company — *Producer:* Dennis Rodbert
THE LARK — *Jean Anouilh*
Mountview Theatre Club — *Producer:* Roger Lawson

List of Productions

CURTMANTLE
  West Cornwall Theatre Group
Christopher Fry
  Producer: Peter Watts

UNDER MILK WOOD
  Northcott Theatre Company
Dylan Thomas
  Producer: Charles Savage

OLIVER
  Bestwood Youth Club
Lionel Bart
  Producer: Alan Tipton

A PENNY FOR A SONG
  Cambridge University Players
John Whiting
  Director: Frank Bechhofer

AND SO TO BED
  The Priory Players
J. B. Fagan
  Producer: Barbara MacRae

*   *   *

Each season's programme is available from Easter. If you would like a copy, please send a stamped addressed envelope to the Manager, Minack Theatre, Porthcurno, Penzance, Cornwall.